Waking Up to Your Worth

Ten Touchstones for Overcoming Imposter Syndrome

By
Jennifer Wilson, MA

Copyright © 2020 by Jennifer Wilson, MA

https://consultnewleaf.com/

All Rights Reserved No part of this publication may be reproduced, distributed, or transmitted in any form or by any means, including photocopying, recording, or other electronic or mechanical methods, without the prior written permission of the publisher, except in the case of brief quotations embodied in critical reviews and certain other noncommercial uses permitted by copyright law.

ISBN: 978-1-7357561-0-3

Publishing Support Services: Motivational M.D.

Publishing https://imreadytolaunch.com

Cover design by Candy Phelps, Bizzy Bizzy.
Author photograph by Beth Skogen Photography

Contents

Dedication   v

Acknowledgements   vii

Introduction   xi

Chapter

    1   Just Believe   1

    2   Develop Discernment   11

    3   Embrace Interdependence   21

    4   Be Generous   37

    5   Learn to Heal   51

    6   Just Surrender   65

    7   Be Brave and Courageous   75

    8   Walk in Integrity   83

    9   Honor Honesty   91

    10   Create Space   107

Conclusion   117

Dedication

To Ashlee and Aurora

I met Ashlee when she was a teenager. She was one of the first students to enroll in a school that I co-founded, and she signed up for the outdoor wilderness adventures that I led. We had both sublime and steaming mad canoe paddles together (she is the best natural paddler I've ever seen). Beneath her surly, cut-you-with-my-words exterior, I recognized an extraordinary soul—determined, smart, empathetic, curious, wise, loving, visionary. I could see her true nature shining through and stayed with her no matter how hard she tried to push me away. She let me know, in her own unspoken way, that maybe she wanted me in her life, and that maybe she needed me.

Ashlee was our first graduating class valedictorian and went on, despite the obstacles in her way, to graduate magna cum laude with a BA in Communications on full scholarship at an HBCU, Alcorn State University. She is a fiercely devoted mother to Aurora, supports many of her family members, owns her own duplex, and is always looking up even when she feels the most down. When I told her I was writing a book about Imposter Syndrome, she said, "What's that?" Exactly why she is my mentor in this regard.

Ashlee, I love you and RaRa deeply. Thank you for being my friend and teacher in this lifetime, as we heal and find freedom, together. Remember the words of the Buddha—no one is more worthy of your love and compassion than yourself.

Acknowledgments

There are many people, known and unknown, who helped this book come to life. I know it is impossible to mention everyone by name, but trust that if you know you touched my life, I know it too.

Thank you to my writing coach, Dr. Jasmine Zapata, for helping me sift through the hill of ideas to find this book that wanted to be written first and for holding me to our production schedule at every step. Thanks also to Sagashus Levingston for living boldly, bravely, and beautifully, and helping other women do the same. Your Infamous Mother's work connected me to Dr. Jaz. You both lit my fire and helped me birth this book that has been gestating for so long. I am grateful for your partnership. Thank you to Lizza Robb for the great gift of your editing expertise, offered with love and generosity. My gratitude and admiration to my reviewers who are outstanding humans and respected leaders in their fields and communities: Nellis Kennedy-Howard, Tim Wortham, Jr., and Mare Chapman.

Many people throughout my life showed me kindness and gave me encouragement when I needed it most.

From my early years, many of whom have passed on: Mrs. Richardson and Mrs. Paul for telling me I could be a writer. Mr. Carter for being the one adult I saw stand up for me to my parents. Mrs. Wenzel for talking with me in your office and having a house full of rambunctious volleyball girls over on a school night. Mr. Rostkowski for insisting on excellence and teaching me a college semester's worth of inorganic chemistry. Ms. Schroeder for opening up the world of literature philosophy to me. Bjørg, for helping me fly away right after graduation to work and live on the Broa with your loving family—a new world in every respect.

Professionally, many women have reached out a hand to help me along: Denise Derdeyn, Jill Boyd, Marleen Pugach, Ronni Ariens, Susan Ballje, Chauna Perry, LaRhonda Bennett, Chris Holmes, Maureen Sullivan, Julie Brown, Laura Page, Julie Andersen, Becca Krantz, Amy Climer, Tina Hallis, Kerry Schumann, Sara Finger, Maury Cotter, Eva Hernandez-Simmons, Becki Clayborn, Robin Mann, Urvashi Vaid, Carla Sutherland, Sloan Leo, Sharon Lezberg, Jen Bailey, Helen Sarakinos, Sarah Shatz, Meg Gaines, Jill Jacklitz, Sarah Davis, Rachel Grob, and Isra Pananon.

Being an independent consultant means you have to create your own team, and I extend deep gratitude to these women for being my friends and confidantes, as well as trusted and talented colleagues: Toral Livingston-Jha, Kim Stezala, Lizza Robb, Sarah Hodgdon. Special acknowledgement to Suzanne Rotondo for your partnership and connecting me to some of my most exciting work. My deepest thanks to every consulting and coaching client I've had for placing your trust in me and helping me grow in ways seen and unseen.

For guiding me along the path to power, self-trust, and integrity: Greg Schneider, Dan Benavides, Robert Gass, Judith Ansara, and Carol Faynik.

For spiritual care, Rodney and Bethany Sanchez and the Tender Shoot of Joy sangha; Mare Chapman and the community of women that gathers in silence and support each December to remember our power and light; Cynthea Jones, Patricia Storm, Rena Bailey, Kay Earley, and many others from the Diana's Grove community; Shaun Perkins, poet and curator of the Rural Oklahoma Museum of Poetry (ROMP).

My biological family made me who I am, for better or worse. I thank my grandparents for their unconditional love, and a special thanks to Grandma for supporting my world travels early on. I remain hopeful that my siblings and their families will reunite—my door is open. Thanks to my stepdaughter Clare for sharing passion for our planet and knowing that toast should be buttered all the way to the edges, and to my in-law family for welcoming me with open arms and hearts.

To my oldest friend, Dan Cone: You saw, you know where I came from. Thank you for rides to the frame shop so I didn't have to drop out of Carroll College and for rescuing me in a blizzard. You were my friend when my self-esteem was on empty and I did stupid things. Thanks for still being my friend.

Friendship helps us remember who we really are. Some friendships last forever, some end for reasons unknown, but I am grateful for them all. You know who you are.

Thank you to these extra bright stars in my friend constellation that make up my "Framily": Ashlee and Aurora; Stacy and Lena and Lauren and Bennett; Lizzi. To Warren and Kevin, Doug and Michael—thank you for the many years of connecting conversations, amazing meals, laugh-until-we-cry hilarities, journeys near and far, and for always being there, with love.

And always, to my husband, Doug, who came to me in a dream and met me on a trail—your faith in me lights the dark. *Seawater begs the pearl to break its shell, and the lily, how passionately it needs some wild darling!* —Rumi

I couldn't have predicted the surprising unfolding of my life's journey—thank you, everyone, for being oases along the way, whistling in the dark, and celebrating in the light.

My friend Elizabeth Dahlk is a writer, educator, and activist who captured the essence of life's unfolding beautifully in this poem:

Possibilities

If on your journey,
Every hill and dale,
Each summit and plateau,
All bogs and briars
Were mapped and drawn,
Would you be where you are now?

Remember, when you meandered
Along an unmarked path,
Unsure at the fork
Which branch to follow,
The instinct that swayed you
Makes you who you are now.

Had you not paused
To turn over a rock,
Gaze at the clouds at twilight,
Listen to the lark's song at dawn,
And discovered their alternate world,
Would you know all you do now?

Like the explorer
Who scans the horizon,
Guided only by her imagination,
Chooses a river valley to explore,
You have charted your course
And perhaps drawn a map for others to follow.

Introduction

My brother and I thought we had moved to a park. We sat astride the cement decorative deer in the backyard and looked around at the quarter acre of yard—the oaks, the weeping willow, the open space that would host hundreds of games of football and softball with the neighborhood kids—and were both giddy and disoriented. We'd come from a tiny starter house in the city, on a street of almost identical houses, so close that we could say goodnight to the girls in the bedroom over, with a postage stamp lawn and an alley to play in. Since we didn't know anything different, it was a fine-sized world, and we had the run of the block, popping in and out of other kids' houses and yards.

In 1976, we packed up and moved—mother, father, baby sister and the two of us—in the Great White Flight to the countryside. I didn't understand it then, but we were part of a migration sparked by the late-in-coming enforcement of school anti-segregation law that scared white people out of Milwaukee. I remember being asked, "Do you want to ride a bus for an hour and go to an all-black school?" I didn't have any bad feelings about that myself at seven-years-old, but I knew the answer I was supposed to give (and as we know, it wasn't the white kids who rode the buses into neighborhoods not their own, sent to learn among strangers). They thought they were doing the right thing as parents for their children, and so that's what we did.

The country neighborhood we lived in was a hodgepodge of lake cottages converted to 4-season homes, clustered around a small and weedy lake. Up the hill, the nice houses stood in even larger yards, spaced far apart in suburban style. Some of the folks up there didn't care to be associated with the folks down the hill, and one woman even started a petition to change the names of the roads to make the distinction clear.

When I was older, I hated living far from town and all of my girlfriends, isolated without a way to get myself to their houses, but as a kid? The beauty of a naturally contained neighborhood, boundaried by highway, lake, roads, and farm fields, was having the run of the place from dawn till dusk. We climbed trees, packed snow into igloos, ice skated, rode dirt bikes, wiped out in gravel and patched up our own wounds, swam, and played baseball, basketball, football until we couldn't see the ball anymore and the fireflies came out. Then we played Ghost in the Graveyard and Kick the Can, hearts racing, skin reeking of bug spray and calamine, feet black with dirt.

So that's the idyllic part, my life outside the house. Inside the house, another story was unfolding. Most people didn't guess or glimpse it, and those that did acted like folks did in those days. They might shake their heads with concern, but it was a private matter, and you didn't interfere in another man's home.

As kids get older, they start comparing stories, and the three of us soon figured out that our home was different. In other homes, the mom didn't drink at 9 am and leave glasses with sticky sweet residue around the house or hide blackberry brandy in a desk drawer. In other homes, the father didn't scream until spit hit your face, enraged over food bits inadvertently left in a sink strainer, large pointer finger bruising your breastbone as it jabbed. In other homes, bookshelves didn't come crashing down in the night and mothers and fathers didn't show up for meals with scrapes and scratches from the latest battle. In other homes, children slept peacefully after lights out and didn't lay tense and alert for the most dreaded sound—the steel toed boots stamping up the stairs. The ceiling light would whip on, glaring over the next barrage of rage over who knew what.

On Sundays, we drove 45 minutes to an affluent church in an affluent suburb where we stood out in our poor clothes, mine often badly homemade, all of us out-of-date except my mother, who bought herself the latest styles. We sat through three hours of church. My father taught Sunday School to little kids, sang in the choir, even stood up and did a solo, singing or on trumpet. No one knew what happened as soon as the car doors closed.

The most insidious thread weaving through my life was something like a shadow, hard to see directly but flickering out of the corner of my eye, an invisible shroud waiting to catch me. *Is it real? Doesn't anyone else see it? Can't someone help me?* were the thoughts that haunted me. My awareness of it started early at age five, on a sunny day when I went into my parents' bedroom to ask a question. My mother was at work—so much happened when she was at work—and my father was napping. I looked, confused, at a naked man. "What's that?" I asked. "That's my puppet. Do you want to see? You can touch it." I remember jerking my hand back in surprise, "It peed on me!" Hearing, "It's okay. Don't tell." And I didn't.

Over the years, my fear and humiliation grew, snaking throughout my body; my heart would literally burn. In high school, my skin turned sticky and gray in the winter months when I could hide it, too afraid to shower for fear of being watched. I'd wash my hair in the sink, wash my hands. I wore baggy clothing to hide my figure. I wasn't allowed to lock a door when I was in the bathroom or my bedroom, but sometimes I risked the consequences and did it anyway. I shrunk and slinked around, keeping to myself and to my room as time went on. Stay quiet, small, and still. Slip under the radar, don't get noticed.

Everything that was already simmering boiled over in 6th grade when my father was fired from his job for exposing himself to a woman who was cleaning the bathroom. We were told he was framed, that no way did he do it, they'd go to court. My brother and I wordlessly communicated with knowing eye contact, yes, he did. They never did go to court. Now, we were thrown into a financial crisis from which we'd never recover, a pressure cooker compressing an already volatile situation. We dreaded asking for anything, even lunch money. "Here, you eat. I guess I won't," as he handed it out. My mother bitterly resented having to return to full-time work and didn't let him or anyone forget it. She'd kick him, he'd kick us. My brother yelled back. I silently swallowed my fear and shame. My sister disappeared into her own world or smashed her toys in nameless rage.

My mother's large green jugs of Gallo rosé piled up faster in the bins. My brother found the stash of porn my father kept under the trash bags in the bins. "Don't tell your mother." We'd watched him steal magazines at the liquor store, sticking them inside his coat while we were supposed to be picking out soda. I watched one of our dogs die, unable to eat because its jaw was broken from a vicious kick of a steel-toed boot, and they were either too poor or too afraid, or both, to take him to the vet.

Then the episodes began, which frightened us more than anything. He wouldn't know who we were, or the way home. His voice would change—he seemed to become a different person, smiling and ingratiating and a stranger to us. When I had to call for a ride home from work or my volleyball match, it took up to 30 minutes on the payphone in the hall, my teammates laughing as I kept repeating, "It's me. It's Jenni. I need a ride. I'm at school." I'd wait alone in the dark, not knowing which version of my father would be driving the car when it finally appeared.

One night, we all came back from the grocery store to find all of the knives laid out on the counter, and his voice calling from the dark, "Go ahead, use them. I know you wish I was dead." There were appointments, a bottle of pills, but nothing was ever explained to us.

One day, during another yelling match, my father charged out of the house and slammed the screen door behind him, catching my pursuing mother on the bridge of the nose. She screamed and fell to the ground, but he didn't look back or stop, and he drove away. There was a lot of blood. She took herself into the bathroom, and eventually emerged and told me she had to go to the hospital. I had my learner's permit and somehow drove us to the nearest hospital, 30 minutes away so she could get stitches. The next day she asked, "Do you think I should get a divorce?" I didn't hesitate. "Yes." She didn't. We didn't talk about what happened again.

But I had saving graces: books, nature, friends, school, and sports. One thing I am grateful for is that we were taken to the library and allowed to check out stacks of books. They became my companions, my escape. So did the woods and meadows and lake around me. I'd pack a lunch and grab a blanket, stick some field guides in my pack, and go read in a meadow, invisible in the tall grass or high up in the branches of a weeping willow, hidden in a curtain of leaves, safe and alone.

In middle school, I connected with a group of friends who came over from the Catholic school that ended at grade 6, and suddenly, I had friends who were smart, who liked me, and liked what I liked. We were the "nerds" who did our homework and cheered each other's good grades. We were in band, we played sports, and we led clubs. We were going to college. Because they were, I could follow along, learning the steps vicariously through them as their parents helped them navigate their way through applications and acceptance letters and financial aid.

Those girls literally saved my life. I knew if I could just hold on until graduation, then I could fly away and find another way to live. I had to believe something better was out there, not just in books. I longed for a life where I wasn't told I was stupid, where I would feel loved. I've heard many people say, "Yeah, they were rough on us, but I know they loved me." I really didn't know that. I thought I was a burden to be endured. I remember watching a happy couple move in next door. I'd hear them laugh, see them having a beer in their cheap lawn chairs at sunset, holding hands. Then one day I saw that she was pregnant, and all I could think was, "Why'd they go and ruin everything?"

My friends had a glimpse once in a while that things were off with my family, but I never told them the extent of my despair. I was too ashamed to let them see how sick and dirty I felt, and hopeless that anyone could help me. *Don't tell...* I tried to spend all of my hours away from home. I'd stay after school to take the late bus home even when my sports weren't in season. I took any babysitting job I could and started washing dishes at 15 to be away and because I knew I'd have to pay my way through college.

When I finally graduated at 17, I got on a plane three days later and flew to Norway with my friend, an exchange student who invited me home to work on her family's ship for the summer. I flew away into the beginning of the rest of my life. I never went back.

We Are Not Our Stories

So I've just told you a story. It's not the whole story, which seems impossible to tell, even if I wrote for the rest of my days. Is it true? I think that depends who you ask. My parents would tell you it's not, and I'm sure everyone in it would tell it differently. But it is the story that is true to me, and it holds the seeds of what would grow into full-fledged depression, incredibly poor relationship choices, and of course, Imposter Syndrome.

Thankfully and blessedly, I have learned that I am not this story. This story is losing its solidity as I grow older and, hopefully, wiser. The past is a dream that is no longer happening, but seems like it happened. What I know today is that the only place that life is really happening is *now*. This moment. Now, this moment.

In this present moment, I'm 51, living a life that I had no capacity to imagine back then. After years of therapy, self-help books, retreats, and hours of meditation practice, I'm better at remembering my essential true and good nature. I more easily believe I'm deserving and worthy of this life, and of dwelling in love and peace. I've forgiven my biological family members and let go of the guilt I used to feel because I escaped, survived, and went on to thrive.

I still rely on many of the same lifelines that saved me as a child: books, nature, friends, athletic pursuits, and now career in place of school. I have a supportive and loving family—my husband, stepdaughter, in-laws, an inner circle of long-time friends. I have a larger circle of trusted friends and colleagues who inspire me and to whom I give what I can. I'm an activist and donor, fighting for racial, social, and environmental justice. I travel to different cultures and seek out wilderness as often as I can, and have even gone on expeditions in the African bush and Antarctica, to witness the beautiful places I seek to protect.

Professionally, I've stayed true to my vision to help make the world a better, safer place for all people. I've co-founded two public schools in Milwaukee, counseled hundreds of teens, led young people into wild places in canoes, on skis, with backpacks. I founded New Leaf Coaching and Consulting LLC in January 2006 and have continued to grow my skills as an organizational development consultant, facilitator, and executive coach. I've worked with national organizations like Sierra Club and The Obama Foundation, as well as local organizations in my community of Madison,

Wisconsin like UNIDOS, REAP Food Group, Center for Patient Partnerships, and Reach Dane.

Starting a school is an endeavor like no other, especially when the school is for students who exist on the margins of traditional public education. Systemic racial oppression, economic disparities, mainstream Christian ideology, and "bootstrap" mentality create whole classes of young people that are discounted, pushed out, or denigrated. I became an outspoken and determined advocate, using my voice, skills, and power to gain support and funding to serve students who many considered to be undeserving. One high school was designed to serve students who were being bullied or harassed for being different in some way—queer, nerdy, gender fluid, goth, large-bodied, quirky, shy, trans—basically not conforming to traditional dominant culture. The other high school served students who experienced a major disruption in their educational journey such as incarceration, illness, mental health crises, or parenthood. Both schools are still open and have provided an educational safe haven for hundreds of students.

Learning how to bring ideas into reality, despite challenges and roadblocks, gave me the courage to realize another dream I had. Becoming an independent consultant and a business owner was the summit of a mountain I'd been eyeing all my adult life. I fought hard to discover confidence in myself and believe that I was smart, talented, skilled, and worthy of someone else's time and money. The business itself wasn't the peak, but internalizing the courage to claim the vision—to see myself standing proudly up there in the thin air, shouting, "Here I am!" As I look back on the path, I see the chain of people who, hand by helping hand, guided me along. No one rises alone.

What is Imposter Syndrome?

Failure is a feeling long before it's an actual result.
—Michelle Obama

I've run a game on everybody, and they're going to find me out.
—Dr. Maya Angelou

Imposter Syndrome—if you've ever felt it, you know what it is. And, you may have felt it but had no name for what you were feeling. I believe in the power of naming things as a first step toward working with our thoughts and feelings, and fortunately, researchers help us name things. The term "Imposter Syndrome" was first coined in the 1970's by clinical psychologists Pauline Clance and Suzanne Imes who observed a puzzling phenomenon among high achieving women: even when there was an abundance of external evidence of success and accomplishment in their lives, these women did not believe that they deserved or rightfully earned the success that they attained. While researchers first discovered this syndrome in women, ongoing study shows that it is pervasive across the gender spectrum. Imposter Syndrome occurs across race, age, occupation, and other demographics and identities, and it often disproportionately affects people belonging to marginalized or underrepresented groups.

I discovered this phenomenon myself in the course of my work. I grew truly alarmed as I witnessed a pervasive and pernicious pattern across groups of women that I coached and facilitated in a variety of settings. These were talented, accomplished, successful, dynamic women of all ages and walks of life, yet across the board, in setting after setting, I saw women struggling with their self-confidence and self-worth. They struggled to see themselves as successful despite all evidence to the contrary.

One exercise in particular brought Imposter Syndrome to light. In the course of a retreat or workshop, I'd instruct the group to take out a piece of paper. "On one side," I'd say, "write down the things that you don't like about yourself or wish you could change." Sometimes, women would laugh and shake their heads as they joked, "Can I have three more sheets?" Pens and pencils would fly over the paper, right up until I called time. Then, I'd instruct them to flip their papers over and list at least ten things they love about themselves—their talents and strengths. The room would go quiet. There were long, thoughtful looks at the ceiling. There was some sighing, with only occasional writing. Shoulders hunched, faces frowned.

Time after time, most women just couldn't do it. They couldn't find ten things they loved, while they had a list of 10, 20, 30, even 40 things they didn't like or accept about themselves.

This felt utterly unacceptable to me. And utterly familiar to me.

In my experience as a friend, coach, and consultant, I know that Imposter Syndrome is like a weed—it can grow in any place, any nook or cranny it can find purchase, anytime, anywhere, in any conditions. I've listened to Executive Directors of huge national organizations who are calm, cool, and collected while testifying to Congress or being interviewed on CNN who privately wonder, "Why the hell is everyone turning to me for answers? As if I know! How am I supposed to pull this off?" I hear it in a teen girl who says, "I really don't know why they picked me. I guess they just felt sorry for me," after winning a lead role in the school play.

One of my most notable experiences of Imposter Syndrome struck me at the very same moment I felt a rush of pride, accomplishment, and gratitude for my life. I was walking down 5th Avenue with the leader of a large national nonprofit after I facilitated a day of strategic planning. We were on our way to join the team at a happy hour, and we were engrossed in a conversation about intersectionality, walking in the hot wind and navigating the New York City sea of pedestrians and traffic. She said, "It's so refreshing to talk with you about this because you get it. I feel like I explain it over and over, and people can't grasp it." You might guess where this is going...

As I kept talking and walking like a normal person on the outside, on the inside, my mind lit up with the thought, "Here I am, just a girl from the cornfields, having a conversation about intersectionality with a powerful woman of color who advises the White House, walking down 5th Avenue—is anyone seeing this?" I was giddy.

The next moment, I was filled with fear of being found out as unequal to the task I was hired to do.

Like a coin flipped in the air, I watched two sides of my self-concept flash back and forth at me in the summer sky: accomplished adult woman / insecure stupid girl.

Imposter Syndrome strikes again.

How to Use this Book

> *touchstone: (def.) as a metaphor, a touchstone refers to any physical or intellectual measure by which the validity or merit of a concept can be tested (Wikipedia).*

I hope this book will be like a box of treasures that you might have kept as a child, full of Touchstones that you can pull out when you're looking for reassurance or inspiration. You can keep this book close at hand, available in moments when Imposter Syndrome kicks in. When that voice—you know the one I'm talking about—starts whispering so convincingly, making its case against you with such convincing logic, you can open this book and reach for the Touchstone you need to challenge the validity or merit of that voice:

Chapter 1: Just Believe
Chapter 2: Develop Discernment
Chapter 3: Embrace Interdependence
Chapter 4: Be Generous
Chapter 5: Learn to Heal
Chapter 6: Just Surrender
Chapter 7: Be Brave and Courageous
Chapter 8: Walk in Integrity
Chapter 9: Honor Honesty
Chapter 10: Create Space

I believe that these Touchstones help us remember and become aware of our true nature. The best thing about our true nature is that it is *who we already are*. We don't have to work, struggle and strain to become a whole, worthy, and deserving soul, but we aren't taught that. Instead, we are taught that we aren't okay the way we are, so we end up doing forced labor in the construction site of our souls, trying to build ourselves up. In reality, our task is to unlearn all the lies we've internalized in order to remember who we truly are—and to wake up to our worth over and over again when we forget.

The first time you read this book, I suggest reading it from start to finish, as some of the stories and concepts build on each other. You'll come to see how each Touchstone is inextricably linked to the others, and the medicine for healing ourselves in these various areas of our lives is often the same. Once you've read all the way through, you can come back again and again to pick up the Touchstone that calls to you at any given moment. You can open this book at random, put your finger on a page, and see what words find you, right where you are. You can gift it to a friend who you want to lift up, or you can discuss it in your book club or circle of friends. There are many ways to find what you need in these pages.

This Book is For All of Us

I wrote this book for me, and I wrote it for you. I wrote it for all of us who have had a 5th Avenue moment. I have had many, and they sneak up on me in both completely predictable and completely surprising moments, like a bolt of lightning on a clear blue-sky day.

Throughout my life, dozens of people have said, "You should write a book and share your story." People most frequently say that when they hear about something horrific from my early years, something they would never have imagined happening to the person they see before them. I wrote it to honor everyone who believed that people could be helped by hearing my story.

I wrote it to illustrate that once upon a time, there was a girl called Jenni who was born whole and innocent, and learned to make herself small to survive. Who was taught her place and her worth by hurting, unwhole people, who did the best they could, which wasn't very good. She swallowed whole the messages she received—that she was unlovable, stupid, and didn't belong.

I wish I could say that those messages stop coming our way when we become adults, but there is no shortage of diminishing messages that are slung our way throughout life, particularly if you are queer, poor, fat, skinny, nonwhite, single, too smart, too sensitive, too anything, or not enough of something that is valued in a consumerist, patriarchal, and racist culture. I recognize the ways in which I am both privileged and disprivileged. I am white, married, and cisgendered, but I'm also buddhist, bisexual, twice-divorced, stepmother, feminist, pro-choice, and other things that put me outside of mainstream U.S. dominant culture.

What I do know is this: Imposter Syndrome is created on the outside, but can only be overcome on the inside.

Our creation stories will differ in the details, in their shape and form. Some of yours, like mine, include classism, homophobia, religious judgement, and misogyny. For some of you, your origin stories include racism. While I cannot, as a white person, know from experience what it is like to navigate a racist world on a daily basis, I know that racism can feed shame, humiliation, lack of confidence, and even self-loathing in a world that is already hard enough to navigate. Racism has created unmitigated environmental, financial, and public health crises that disproportionately harm and kill people of color, and dehumanize us all.

While our stories are very personal, we don't need to have lived another's life to have our hearts reach out with compassion for another's pain. In the words of Archbishop Desmond Tutu, "My humanity is bound up in yours, for we can only be human together." Your story is my story, and my story is your story, for all of us can find in ourselves a glimmer of recognition—the cruel words, the raised hand, the contemptuous slur, the looks of disdain, the feeling when we receive the message loud and clear that *you don't belong*.

These experiences are the birthplace of the Imposter who continues to grow up, fed and kept alive with the stories we continue to believe and tell ourselves, about ourselves.

Let me repeat this concept: overcoming Imposter Syndrome is an inside job.

Many years ago, I heard a parable that has stayed with me. An aikido master was talking with his students, and one of them admiringly said, "Master, you never lose your balance!" He replied, "I lose my balance all the time. I just recover more quickly." My hope is that this book will help all of us recover more quickly and, ultimately, let the internal voice of our Imposter Syndrome fade away like a song we used to know by heart, but no longer sing.

Until then, while the Imposter's voice is still hanging around, let's welcome it as a wise teacher. Let's invite it to sit down for a cup of tea so we can get to know what it's all about and what it has to say to us, with curiosity and love. When we've heard all we need and there's nothing more to the story that's news to us, we can bid it, "Thank you, and farewell." Until then, we have these Touchstones to help us along the way.

CHAPTER ONE

Just Believe

Go find a mirror right now. As you look in it, place your right hand, palm facing out, just behind your right ear. Now turn away from the mirror—can you see it? Look back in the mirror. Plain as day, right? Turn away, and it disappears.

Other people can serve as our mirrors when our Imposter Syndrome keeps us from seeing ourselves clearly. Someone else looking at you can see the hand behind your ear plain as day, and they can say, "Hey, you have a hand up behind your ear."

Our attributes, skills, and talents can be like that hand. You'd think we'd know they're there because they are as much a part of ourselves as our own hand, but Imposter Syndrome blinds us to them. We literally can't see them at times. Although we can readily see and admire other people's talents, when something comes effortlessly to us, we're prone to discount it as no big thing rather than recognize talent in ourselves.

This is where the Touchstone of Just Believe comes in

When we hear someone say, "I see your (strength, skill, talent, ability, potential)", we have a choice (and in every moment, we always have this choice). We can discount it and not believe them—score one for Imposter Syndrome—or we can Just Believe.

While it's intellectually quite easy to see how the first option is self-limiting and the second option is self-affirming, it's not so easy in practice to live into the second choice. Why? What's happening in those moments, quick as lighting?

The Voice of Imposter Syndrome

When someone tells us that we're talented, or skilled, or full of potential to do something, we don't usually come out and say, "You are lying." Well, some of us might. What I usually do is flip it around onto myself and start speaking fluently in the language of Imposter Syndrome. Here's how that looks and sounds.

Let's start with writing this book. I've had a hundred people—maybe more?—tell me, "You should write a book!" throughout my life. It's happened so often that I now laugh when someone says it yet again. They look at me with confusion and ask, "Why are you laughing?" I tell them, "Oh, I hear that all the time." Sometimes they reply, "Well, then maybe you should." Sometimes, they just change the topic.

What relief! My Imposter Syndrome laughter effectively stopped the exchange in its tracks. We could move off that topic, even though inside, my heart was leaping with delight that this person said the very words I long to hear. If you're thinking, "Wow, that sounds contradictory and confusing," you're right on—that's exactly how it feels.

Once in a while, some brave soul would push on, and then we'd get into a back and forth that mostly consisted of them making supportive suggestions and me providing well-rehearsed and rational reasons why I was just not going to write a book, or why I wanted to write a book but probably wouldn't, or why I would write a book someday but couldn't now, and you get the idea.

I'm going to let you eavesdrop and hear what my Imposter Syndrome sounds like in those moments—and sounds like even now, as I'm sitting here *actually writing the book*.

- *Who would want to read what I have to say? It's not like I'm famous.*
- *There are enough books in the world already.*
- *People will think it's not very good, then judge me and my abilities as not very good.*
- *It doesn't have extensive academic research in it, so people will dismiss it.*
- *People will critique it, find it wanting, poke holes in it. They'll criticize me as an author. Who needs that?*
- *I don't want to be the object of people's pity or sound like I'm blaming all my problems on a rough childhood.*
- *It won't be Oprah Book Club worthy.*
- *There are so many masterful teachers already. Why add my voice when they've said it all already?*
- *I don't want to sound whiny or preachy, or like I have the answers.*

This is what I was telling myself on the inside. What came out of my mouth was a bunch of excuses—how busy I was, how I couldn't stand to be on the computer any more hours in the day, how many clients I had demanding my time—all driven by the voice that was essentially saying, "You're not good enough to write a book, and even if you did, no one except your friends would buy it." It didn't matter if they told me that I had talent as a writer, or how much my blog post spoke to them, or how my story of overcoming abuse and trauma inspired them—to go on a solo journey, or say yes to a job that scared them, or move across the country, or break off a bad relationship.

Your Imposter Syndrome Isn't Just Your Problem

This next point is hugely important. We need to understand that Imposter Syndrome is damaging and limiting not only to ourselves, but to the people around us who may also struggle with Imposter Syndrome.

When we don't believe a person's assessment of us, we're essentially telling them that they're wrong. We are telling them to question their own thinking and ability to draw intelligent conclusions. We are rejecting their thoughts that they were generous and brave enough to share, and we often silence them. We become complicit in creating conditions that can feed their own self-doubt and make them question their decision to speak their truth.

I doubt this is what we intend, but that is our impact. Imposter Syndrome, unhealed, wants nothing more than for others to be less than powerful and confident, too. It keeps us all staying small, playing small.

What Happens When We Just Believe

Fortunately, not everyone falls for this act, and I hope that, like me, you have encountered people who decided not to accept your opinion of their assessment of you. There have been crossroads in my life when I took an unimagined and blessed turn, and always, there is a person—usually another woman—standing there with an open hand and heart. By some grace, I've had people in my life who believed in me when I didn't believe in myself. And by grace, I decided to believe them.

One woman is Dr. Marleen Pugach, Professor Emerita at University of Wisconsin-Milwaukee, who literally wrote the book about *Why Teaching Matters*. Back in January 2006 when I launched my business, I was living in an attic apartment upstairs from friends, temporarily renting the flat between tenants, sitting at a card table with my laptop and a cup of tea, and having not a clue about how it would all go. I no longer had my educator's monthly income and benefits to rely on, so I decided that my financial goal was to earn enough money for rent and expenses just one month at a time. While I was short on cash, I was rich with elation each time a bit of work came in to move me closer to my goal. One day, a call came from Marleen. She told me that an instructor was suddenly unable to teach an intro level course for Education majors, and she wanted to see if I could teach it. It started in one week.

My Imposter Syndrome was in pretty high gear in those days, and instead of smoothly saying, "Interesting. Tell me more," I awkwardly blurted out something like, "Oh, I've never taught a college class so I don't think I can do that, but thanks for asking. I really don't think I can."

After a pregnant pause, she said with complete self-assurance and calm confidence, "Jennifer, if I didn't think you could do it, I wouldn't have asked you." She went on to tell me why she thought I was qualified and capable, and asked again if I would accept an adjunct faculty position and teach the course.

I thank myself for having the wisdom and courage to Just Believe her, and I said, "Yes."

That decision was one of the best of my life, and I taught joyfully for two years, until my consulting practice filled and I shifted my energy to that work. I was one of the highest-rated instructors of that course, and my experiential techniques were emulated by several of my colleagues. I still hear from some of my students from time to time, seeking advice or letting me know how they're doing. Some of them have told me that I was the best teacher they'd ever had, and they try to teach the way I'd taught them.

So if it's true that the cost of giving in to Imposter Syndrome hurts not only ourselves, but potentially those around us, then overcoming it elevates not only ourselves, but also those around us. I'm lucky that I got to hear this feedback because we often don't know the impact we have. When we say "Yes" to someone who believes in us, we say "Yes" to the well-being of all who cross our paths.

Claiming Our Talents and Abilities

One of my mentors, the teacher, writer, and philosopher Cynthea Jones, defines talent as, "What you do well, that I can't." Let that sink in for a minute. Does it ring true for you? It sure did for me the first time I heard it over a decade ago. It can be incredibly hard for us to see our own talents clearly. Our disbelief of our own talent is the mental equivalent of, "What, this old shirt? Had it for years," when someone compliments our outfit. Something that comes easily and is so normal to be able to do can't be talent because we've been misinformed that talent requires blood, sweat, and tears to develop. We mistake talent for discipline, which is showing up for your talent and paying it the respect of commitment and hard work.

When we choose to see ourselves clearly and believe in our own talents, strengths, and abilities, we've cleared one of the biggest hurdles our Imposter Syndrome sets before us. What allows us to continue to have confidence in ourselves is having discipline to do our best in any situation we find ourselves in. I'm not saying we should be perfect (that's another Imposter Syndrome trap to overcome, which we'll talk about in Chapter 6).

Don Miguel wrote a powerful and practical book you may have heard of called *The Four Agreements*. The four agreements are:

Agreement 1: Be Impeccable With Your Word
Agreement 2: Don't Take Anything Personally
Agreement 3: Don't Make Assumptions
Agreement 4: Always Do Your Best

The fourth agreement, *Always do your best*, is his favorite. He says, "The first three exist in our mind. But with action we make it real." The more we do our best and develop our abilities and talents through discipline and practice, the easier it becomes to believe in ourselves and loosen the grip of Imposter Syndrome.

Living Life Without Regret

> *There are more scary things inside, than outside.*
> —Toni Morison, Paradise

When we Just Believe, we allow ourselves to live an *expanded* rather than a *contracted* life. I believe that regret comes from letting opportunities go by—from not leaping, not trying, not finding out what might have been possible.

I spent my 40th birthday riding in a van full of young men from one of the high schools I co-founded in Milwaukee. We were headed up to the northwoods of Wisconsin to spend a few days on a canoeing expedition as part of an experiential program I developed to reconnect urban youth with the natural world and their place in it. My trip co-leader and I happened to share the same birthdate, and it came out that we were both celebrating our birthdays. The guys made a game out of guessing our ages, and I'll admit that it was gratifying how far off they were, never guessing mine correctly. When the whooping and hollering died down once I told them, one young man, a deep-thinking philosophical soul as many of the guys were, said, "Miss Jennifer, most people act all old and like they're afraid to turn forty, but you don't seem that way. How come?"

I told them that I couldn't say why others were afraid, but that for me, forty held no fear because I didn't leave opportunity on the table. I was blessed to have a number of older women friends who were respected elders and teachers in my life. Many of them expressed regret that they didn't start asking, "What do I want? What are my dreams?" until they were 50, 60, 70. I learned from their stories and started believing in myself enough to do big, audacious things, even when my Imposter Syndrome kicked in and I was afraid. I was more afraid of regret than I was of finding out I'd fail. My advice to the vanload of young men was to not wait for "someday" because none of us are guaranteed a someday, and sometimes someday never comes—all we have for sure is today.

I went on to tell them that, in fact, the only reason we were sitting in the van together was because I persevered and didn't give up on my vision for their school, which was to find a way to retain the hundreds of students we lost each year when they returned from incarceration or other major disruptions in their education. Many people at the time told me that it couldn't be done, that the district leaders and Board would never support my vision. I actually quit my job with an educational technical assistance group tasked with creating small schools and gave up a comfortable salary because I had to see my dream through. I convinced the Director of Innovation that this was an idea worth backing, which he did wholeheartedly. Together, we ultimately won the Board's approval with a unanimous vote.

That school is still open and has touched hundreds of lives. The woman to whom this book is dedicated, Ashlee Bishop, was the valedictorian of our first graduating class. None of it would have happened if I hadn't persevered.

The World Needs You

When you Just Believe, you get to find out what can happen. When you give in to Imposter Syndrome, you just get more of the same, and you live with regret. Marianne Williamson, author, political activist, and spiritual thought leader, wrote the following poem in her book, *A Return to Love*. She beautifully illustrates why believing in yourself serves not just yourself, but everyone around you.

Our Deepest Fear

Our deepest fear is not that we are inadequate.
Our deepest fear is that we are powerful beyond measure.
It is our light, not our darkness
That most frightens us.

We ask ourselves
Who am I to be brilliant, gorgeous, talented, fabulous?
Actually, who are you not to be?
You are a child of God.

Your playing small
Does not serve the world.
There's nothing enlightened about shrinking
So that other people won't feel insecure around you.

We are all meant to shine,
As children do.
We were born to make manifest
The glory of God that is within us.

It's not just in some of us;
It's in everyone.

*And as we let our own light shine,
We unconsciously give other people permission to do the same.
As we're liberated from our own fear,
Our presence automatically liberates others.*

The world needs *you* to Just Believe.

Touchstone Practice: Just Believe

Here are some reflection questions to help you discover when you're most and least likely to Just Believe in yourself. No one will see your responses but you, so be as honest as you can, even if it feels uncomfortable.

1. How do you respond when you receive compliments from people? Do you accept them with gratitude? Deflect or deny them? Do you respond differently to some people than others? Why might that be?
2. Think about someone who you admire and inspires you. What specifically do you respect and appreciate about them?
3. Still thinking about that same person, recall a time when they made a mistake or seemed to fail at something. Notice if you have less admiration or respect for them. Now, think about a time when you made a mistake or failed at something. Did you have less admiration or respect for yourself? Notice if there is a difference between how you judge others compared to how you judge yourself.
4. Recall a time when you almost gave up on something or turned down an opportunity, but you didn't. What helped you not give up? What were you thinking and believing about yourself when you decided to persevere?

CHAPTER TWO

Develop Discernment

*Change the story and you change perception;
change perception and you change the world.*
—*Jean Houston*

Imagine being outside on a blustery night, looking up at clouds moving across the sky. You see a faint glow of light, and you guess that the moon is there, hidden from view. Suddenly the clouds part and you see the moon in all its brilliance for a shining moment, and just as quickly, it is obscured by the next billow of clouds. Even though you can no longer see it, you know the moon is still there, and you keep looking for it to appear again.

Seeing our true nature clearly is a bit like looking for the moon in a windy, cloudy sky. When the clouds cover the moon, we don't think that the moon is lost from the sky. We have faith that it endures, even when we could just as easily conclude it doesn't exist. Our true nature is the moon, our mind is the sky, and our thoughts and beliefs and perceptions are the clouds. Clouds will blow by, and the moon remains, unchanged. We have thoughts—sometimes dark thoughts—but our true nature shines on, untouched and unchanged, waiting to be seen when we once again have a clear view.

Cultivating this clear view and having faith in the stable presence of our true, good nature helps us overcome Imposter Syndrome. Seeing your thoughts for what they are--only passing clouds–is discernment.

Developing Discernment: What Gets in the Way

The dictionary definition of this beautiful word is: *the quality of being able to grasp and comprehend what is obscure.*

We have expressions for the challenge of discernment. We say, "His judgement was clouded," or "There's a dark cloud hanging over her," or "They've got their heads in the clouds."

In our personal sky, one major source of clouds is the opinions and judgements of others—or more accurately, what we imagine other people's opinions and judgements of us to be. Rather than letting the clouds blow on by, we catch and hold on to them as if they are solid. In time, our vision is so clouded that we have a hard time seeing what is true.

One of my father's choice expressions was, "You might be an A student, but you can't think your way out of a paper bag." My young brain couldn't make literal sense out of this expression as a kid (partly because he was saying it wrong), but there was no mistaking the meaning—the kind of smart your teachers say you are doesn't matter, because in the ways that matter to me, you're stupid.

The center of my chest literally burned whenever I heard those words. I would hang my head, round my shoulders, and make myself as small as I felt. I know now that what I was feeling was shame. The awful part for me then was that I didn't know what to do differently to change his opinion of me. Worst of all, I didn't know not to believe him.

Another expression I heard often from both of my parents was, "Who do you think you are?" This was a rhetorical question that was not actually a question, but a judgement spoken with contempt. Again, the meaning of the words didn't matter because the message was crystal clear—who you are is not worth much.

From that and many other experiences with family and peers in my youth, I started a decades-long habit of desperately trying to figure out who other people wanted me to be, so they would like me and so I'd be safe. I developed the habit of believing what other people said about me, both good and bad. When I got an A and a teacher told me I was smart, I clung to that A as proof that I was worth something. I worked and worked for those A's, ending up with a 4.3 gpa and graduating third in my class. Wouldn't that prove I was smart?

When a pack of girls on the basketball team bullied me from middle school all the way through high school, I took that as information about myself, too. I don't know if I could have put it into these words then, but I definitely got the message that there must be something really wrong with *me* since they didn't treat my friends that way.

Welcoming Opportunities to Practice

I want to stop right there and tell you the thoughts and feelings I'm having right now.

It feels uncomfortably vulnerable and hard to share these stories. As I write, I feel sad, and my thinking is muddy. Often when I write, the words just fly from my fingertips onto the screen. Today, they are dribbling out, like they've slogged ten miles through a field of muck, emerging tired and bedraggled. I'm noticing that I'm slumped in my chair. This is the impact that Imposter Syndrome has on us energetically. We are sapped of our emotional and intellectual strength when we allow the judgements of others to slice into our souls.

Why do this to myself? I resisted writing about my life for exactly this reason. I didn't want to relive these moments and risk your judgement or your pity. It's true that I've been afraid of being misunderstood or judged. I don't want people to conclude that I'm blaming others for my own troubles, not taking responsibility for my life choices, or fishing for sympathy.

Ah, hello, my old friend, Imposter Syndrome. Your voice has been with me my whole life. I hear you worrying about what other people will think, urging me to stay silent, convincing me it's just not worth it.

You may be surprised to know that while I don't enjoy this feeling, I have learned to welcome and not resist it. What a wonderful opportunity to continue to Develop Discernment and learn to see more clearly!

In this moment, I know to rise out of my chair as a way to interrupt what I'm thinking and feeling. I know to take a deep breath and get curious, so I can consciously see these feelings for what they are—old habits of mind that have nothing to do with my true nature. I remind myself that nothing I remember from the past is happening right now. In this moment, I breathe deeply, ground my feet on the floor, and calmly bring myself back out of the dream of the past into the reality of the present moment by becoming aware of my body. With great tenderness and compassion, I allow these old thoughts and voices to blow away in the wind, like clouds across the sky.

Laying New Neural Pathways

I just took the lid off and let you look inside my mind to illuminate how my mind works and the kinds of maladaptive neural pathways that can get laid in our brains early in life.

There are many informative books, podcasts, and articles about brain science which are really helpful for gaining a deeper understanding of how we develop mental habits and how to change them. Without getting too technical, what we know is that when neurons in our brain communicate and connect with each other in a certain way repeatedly over time, a neural pathway is formed. This is the basis of both learned skills, like being able to tie your shoes without thinking about it, and cognitive/emotional reactions like feeling shame after making even a small mistake. If we had repeated experiences, or an exceptionally strong and vivid incident, of being shamed and criticized when we were young for making mistakes, we are likely to develop neural pathways that strongly link "mistake" with "feel shame" or "angry" with "keep quiet."

The good news is that with conscious effort and practice, we can change our neural pathways. We can Develop Discernment and literally reshape and retrain our brains.

Cherished mentors of mine, Robert Gass and Judith Ansara, liken our conditioned neural pathways to cross country ski tracks laid in the snow. When you ski on a groomed trail, there are tracks that your skis fit in, and you glide along easily in them, on top of even the deepest snow. If you hop out of the tracks into fresh, untracked territory, the going is much harder as you plow your way, slowly forging new tracks. It takes conscious effort and work to develop new mental habits and resist sliding back into well-worn grooves. The going may be easier, but the places they take us are nowhere we want to keep visiting.

Imposter Syndrome is full of beautifully groomed tracks that keep us gliding unconsciously along, directing us over familiar and well-established terrain that we were led into, usually long ago. They have trail names such as Not Smart Enough, Just Lucky, They're All More Qualified than Me, or You Don't Have a PhD.

We can learn to hop out of the old tracks and into fresh fields of snow, where we can feel new feelings, think new thoughts, and make new choices. When we Develop Discernment, we begin to see the old rutted pathways for what they are, and we free ourselves to create new patterns and possibilities.

Learn to Discern

When we have discernment, it's like we have a lie detector built into our brains that keeps us from getting confused and forgetting that we are already whole and well just as we are.

I should probably take a moment to explain that the lies we're trying to detect are any statements or judgements that we or others make about who we are, not what we do.

When people comment on what we do, that's called feedback. We can and should use discernment when we get feedback, too. Sometimes feedback is valid. When someone tells me, "You know, it was hard for me to follow your directions in the last exercise we did. I think it would help if you slowed down, repeated them, and had them on the handout," that is information about my actions, and it's actually quite helpful. It is not information about who I am as a person.

However, this is the kind of material that Imposter Syndrome eats for breakfast. Run through the filter of Imposter Syndrome, that same feedback comes spewing out in our brains as, "Hey, you're supposed to be this great facilitator, when actually, you're such a fraud that you ruined my whole experience. Why the heck they hired you, I don't know. You shouldn't be leading us because you, frankly, suck."

Am I exaggerating? Maybe a bit, for effect. But maybe not. Think about it. Can you recall a time when your mind provided you with a similar translation when someone offered feedback? Maybe the words weren't the same, but your translation may have been just as harsh and damning as this one, and became about who you are and your actual worth. Hello, voice of Imposter Syndrome.

Discernment helps us become better at noticing how often (hint: more often than you think!) we make up stories about what we believe we are hearing others say. Discernment helps us have our minds blown, in a good way, when we start recognizing that it is our beliefs that create our reality.

So what if someone actually does say something that sounds like they are judging who we are? If they actually say, "You're a horrible person"? Discernment helps us in those situations, too.

Let's work with another example that has a lot more emotional load to it, and is a true story.

When I started dating as a newly single person in 2005, one of the first people I dated was a quiet, sensitive introvert who, like me, appreciated really long hikes and the solitude of nature, and he had a beautiful dog who adored me. We were a good fit in many respects, except for one thing—he really didn't like talking, and he disliked me talking or wanting to talk with him even more.

At one point, when he was thinking about calling things off, he wrote in an email to me, "I find myself holding back from and not wanting to share an observation or talk about a topic because I know and can hear in my head what you're going to say. You'll have some knowledge about it already, and I'll end up feeling silly for bringing it up, or like I have the wrong ideas about it. A little bit of humility is refreshing."

With my approval-seeking neural grooves highly activated, I took 100% responsibility for his thoughts and feelings (this is also called codependence, and that is a topic for another book). I felt crushed. Imposter Syndrome kicked in, and I wondered how I could be so wrong as to think I was a humble person who just enjoyed good conversation when all along, I was an arrogant ass who shamed her boyfriend into silence. That was not who and how I wanted to be!

However, I was growing and healing, so a small, brave voice piped up and said, "Excuse me, but could it just be him?" You may have heard the saying, "If one person calls you an ass, let it go. If three people call you an ass, start looking for a tail." So I thought I'd ask—am I an ass?

I chose several trusted women friends who I knew would be 100% honest with me and wrote this email:

Dear friends,

I need a reality check...

A person awfully close to me had this to say (I pasted the message above). I'll share who it was later since I don't want that to bias your reply.

Feedback is a tricky thing, I think. It is information to consider and learn what I can from it, and it is also information about the person giving it. If there's a lesson here for me to learn, I want to find it and grow from it.

As women whose opinion I trust, what do you think about this? If you have time to respond to me, I'd sure appreciate your thoughts and know that whatever you have to say comes from a place of caring. My belief is that I'm sharing what I know out of a desire to communicate, to have an exchange, and to learn more about the topic at hand. Do you experience me as lacking humility when I talk about things? If there's truth here, I need and want to face that.

Love,

Jen

Here are some of the messages I received in reply:

You have my respect for bringing this up. I have never thought that you were showing off your knowledge or were lacking humility.

Trust me when I say that you do not lack humility. You do not treat others as if they are less than you. You do not fit this description that this person has created for you, at all.

I didn't know whether to laugh or feel extremely irritated at that person's quote because it certainly does not describe you! I have never felt those things about you. If anything, you are one of the most effective listeners I know, providing feedback in a non-threatening, thought-provoking, sensitive, and affirming manner. I would suspect that this individual is somehow threatened/jealous of you and your strengths.

I'm bewildered by this person's feedback, particularly because my experience in our interactions doesn't reflect it at all.

You're an excellent listener, always take me seriously, and never condescend. I don't think you've ever responded to me with information in a way that intimated you thought I should already know or that I had the wrong idea.

I stopped looking for my ass' tail, and I lovingly ended our relationship (although you'll get to hear from him again in Chapter 9). I didn't want to be with someone who needed me to silence myself, especially after working so hard to find my voice.

As this story demonstrates, discernment requires us to slow down, get really curious, and question our thoughts and beliefs that feel oh-so-real and true. Asking for help from those we know and trust to tell us the truth is one way we can seek discernment when we're feeling confused.

I don't have any time to stay up all night worrying about what someone who doesn't love me has to say about me.
—Viola Davis

Touchstone Practice: Develop Discernment

I've found that I need other people in order to fully Develop Discernment in my life. Here are some ideas of how to engage with other people to help you practice this Touchstone:

1. Work with a life coach, executive coach, or therapist to help you see your mental and emotional habits more clearly.
2. Ask people who have your best interest at heart for reality checks and honest feedback.
3. Read personal growth books or listen to podcasts on topics that spark your interest. Learn more about neural pathways, habits, and ways we can change them.
4. Find an insight meditation group in your community or one that meets virtually.
5. Explore The Work by Byron Katie to learn how to question what you are thinking and believing.
6. Join a Mastermind Group to help yourself and others grow and be successful.
7. Get involved in a spiritual or religious community that fits with your beliefs and values.
8. Participate in a book club or art/theater/dance discussion group to explore how people throughout the ages and from different cultures have grappled with the challenges inherent in being human.

CHAPTER THREE

Embrace Interdependence

We are made for goodness. We are made for love. We are made for friendliness. We are made for togetherness. We are made for all of the beautiful things that you and I know. We are made to tell the world that there are no outsiders.
—*Archbishop Desmond Tutu*

The lesson of Interdependence may be one of the hardest lessons I've had to learn. It has taken me years to unlearn the habits I developed and cultivate trust in my ability to be in authentic relationship with others while feeling safe and at ease. I can tell you—and the people who love me could tell you—that I'm still learning.

The story I carried in my head and heart for much of my life—as a way to make sense of my unpredictable and violent childhood—was that other people will always let you down, so it's best not to count on them at all. Considering that's the belief I had, then it makes sense that I tried, consciously and unconsciously, not to depend on other people for anything. Brick by brick, I built my tower of independence, only to discover that the bricks that protected me from hurt and pain and disappointment also kept me from experiencing love and connection and nurturing.

Being overly independent has profound effects on our personal lives, and those effects carry over into our professional lives. Imposter Syndrome thrives in the dark and in isolation. When we keep ourselves locked up tight in safe fortresses of independence, it's much harder to have—let alone hear—trusted companions who can keep our feet on the ground and provide a counter-narrative to the lies our Imposter Syndrome would have us believe.

When I was in my late twenties, I worked in settings where there were a lot of mothers and fathers of teen or college age kids, I felt like someone removed a blindfold I didn't realize I was wearing. These people had their kids' college schedules taped inside their planners, so they knew what their days were like and the best times to call. They attended not only their kids' home games but drove to other towns to watch away games, even if their kids weren't starters and sat on the bench. They put together and sent care packages filled with their kids' favorite treats, and they knew what they liked. They helped them pay for college in whatever way they could, whether that was a lot or a little. Watching these parents, it fully dawned on me that most 17-year-olds were not left totally on their own, without financial help or emotional support, like I was.

My survival tactic as a young adult was, out of necessity, "I can take care of myself." As a result, I missed out on a lot of opportunities for support, friendship, and mentoring from my peers and professors. I just didn't know how to ask for, look for, or receive kindness or guidance. I only accepted help when I thought I had no other options, and then I would retreat back into my self-protective shell as soon as I could. I strongly believed not just "If you want something done right, do it yourself," but the even more distorted belief that, "Anything that needs to be done, I have to do it myself."

And here's the thing—this kind of independence is often rewarded in the United States.

Competition and The Myth of the Self-Made Person

For many of us, it begins early in life, in school. If you're my age of 51 or older, you probably remember being graded on a curve. (If you're younger, you may have also had this experience, and it could perhaps be my own optimism that leads me to believe the curve is a relic of the past in education—but I may be wrong about that.) The bell curve, by design, dictates that only a few people can get the highest grades, and conversely, it demands that other people must get the very lowest grades. We were thrown into competition with each other, whether we liked it or not. The curve didn't care if you helped someone figure out the tricky equation at the end of Chapter Eight or if you did flashcards of science terms with your friend until midnight the night before the final. When the test came around, you were on your own. There wasn't room on the curve for everyone to stand side-by-side. We learn competition, not collaboration, early and often.

In the United States, our cultural mythology about the "self-made man," "lone wolf," and "rugged individualist" runs deep, and our work cultures generally reward those who stand out, lead the charge, and get their name on the project. We compete for promotions, to make partner, to win Employee of the Month, to get the highest sales. Competition extends outside of the world of work, too. If we're mothers, let me tell you, the Mom Olympics is a thing. There's someone who uses cloth diapers when you use disposable. Someone else makes their own organic baby food, which you hear about as you surreptitiously fish a Gogurt out of the diaper bag. The language of women's magazines is peppered with headlines that remind us that we're competing to be the best, right down to our literal toenails: "Be Your Best Beach Self," "Top Five Ways to Look Younger than Your Friends," and "Come Out on Top: Tips for Winning at Work."

I was one of the lucky ones who excelled at traditional education and loved a good bell curve. The guys I grew up with from my neighborhood were mostly beaten down by it. I knew it wasn't fair, but I was sharp enough to see that I could save myself and escape this life by getting scholarships to college. It didn't end there, of course. Once I started working, just like in school when I did A work, I got recognized and rewarded for putting in long hours and driving myself too hard, not for taking care of myself. Like many women who juggle marriage, career, and home, I literally did it all (and my ex-husband happily let me). I wound up feeling proud and competent yet profoundly exhausted and resentful, which is a potent recipe for depression and a sure-fire way to sour a relationship.

I'd learned my lessons well. I didn't know what else to do or how else to be.

The Nature of Interdependence

As I came to learn, the other way to be is called interdependence. I now have a deep conviction that whether we believe it or not, we just *are* interdependent. Nothing in this world—not a pebble or a pound cake or a poodle—exists independently of anything else. There are many books about this topic, so I won't get into either the actual physics or metaphysics that support this belief, but I'm going to suggest holding it as true for the purposes of this exploration.

When we seek to recognize our innate interdependence, we are mindfully and consciously acknowledging and aligning with our profound human need to be in relationship.

We know that babies who are not touched or held literally die—they fail to thrive. We are designed to be social. When we feel a sense of connection and belonging, we are more at ease. When we feel alone and isolated, we experience dis-ease.

When we strive to be healthily interdependent, our ego is relaxed and secure enough to acknowledge that everything we've accomplished came about through a web of relationships and interconnected events far too complex and unknowable for us to even comprehend. We come to recognize that it's actually impossible to be an imposter because everything in our lives has conspired to place us exactly in this seat, exactly at this table. We wake up to the fact that asking, "Do I deserve to be here?" is fundamentally the wrong question. We discover instead that the question to ask is, "I am seated here. Who can I thank and who can I help?"

We Are All on the Same Team

Just over fifteen years ago, I was part of a founding team of educators who started a school. It was an endeavor that no one person could have done on their own, and every person on the co-founding team played a part in bringing a vision to life. But you won't find our names listed anywhere as a founding team. Over time, despite our school being founded on values of community and interdependence, we learned that the person who had the initial seed of the idea that grew into our school enjoyed the limelight and wasn't willing to share it with the rest of us who stayed behind the scenes, sharing the workload.

She took the title of Lead Teacher, but in practice, she and I shared that role and the responsibilities that went with it. While others on the founding team did a ton of work, the two of us led the work. I put in 14-16 hour days. I went to homes to recruit students and meet the families of those already enrolled. I built our master schedule. I stood on a staircase in a mansion and asked people to dig deep and write big checks. I was responsible for our phone line and responded to all callers within 24 hours as part of our commitment to excellent parent and student service. I went back out to homes, looking for those who missed our first week of school, reminding them that they mattered to us. Because I had been working in central administration for a few years, I'd developed a strong network of relationships built on being kind and providing excellent service and support. These relationships and my reputation helped open doors and move things along more rapidly when we needed help. I understood every part of the district's electronic school and student information system because I helped launch and train hundreds of staff, and I trained our team, including our school secretary who was brand new to the system. But on paper, my title was School Counselor.

After too many frustrating incidents where I wasn't allowed to authorize things I was responsible for, I told her I wanted to have the title of Co-Lead Teacher, following a model that another start-up school was using successfully. I needed official authority of title that matched my actual roles and responsibilities, particularly when I was conducting school business. She refused and said, "It would confuse the staff." When I suggested we bring the idea to the staff for input since they already saw us as Co-Leads, she refused to put it on our agenda. When I asked to have coffee with her to talk about our work relationship, she showed up with her girlfriend and claimed that she thought it was a social coffee. I carried on, increasingly frustrated and disenchanted with the lack of integrity between the values we publicly claimed and the private reality.

A few months later, I was offered a job by a national organization I'd worked with during my central office tenure that would allow me to work remotely. Suddenly, I had the means to fulfill my dream of moving to Oregon, a place I'd come to love and where I could live the mountain life—backpacking, rock climbing, and mountain biking. When I told her I wanted to take it and move, she blanched. The first thing she said was, "Aren't you worried about what people will think?" When she told me that I would be letting everyone down, including the students, I felt emotionally manipulated. How could I do this to her, and to the staff who needed me? To the students who loved me? How could I quit on everyone?

Her words triggered an old, familiar voice in my head, and I started having doubts. *Who do you think you are?* The voice of shame grew louder, and I felt terrible guilt. The little girl from the cornfields, the good A+ student who desperately wanted people to value her, grew frightened. Despite being a grown woman with a list of professional accomplishments, I was desperate for people to think well of me, to the point that I considered letting my life dream go by.

By some grace, I realized that I couldn't navigate this on my own. I needed someone to help me. I went to our most level-headed staff member, someone who lived authentically and had a secure sense of self, and told him about my dilemma. He listened, then smiled and laughed, lightly and kindly. "Jen," he said, "don't worry. We'll be fine. We'll be just fine."

That helped, more than he could know. I went ahead with my plans, but on the day when I stood in front of our student body to break the news, I was still full of guilt. I was afraid of facing their disappointment or their anger, of hearing, "You're a fake—you don't love us after all." As I choked out some rambling words about needing to follow your dreams in life, the light of realization dawned in one young woman's eyes. "Hey," she exclaimed, "she's telling us she's leaving."

I burst into tears and started sobbing, and immediately, the young people said, "What's wrong? What's wrong?" and half-rose out of their seats with concern. I said, "I'm so afraid I'm letting you down and disappointing you." Their faces instantly shifted from anxious worry to broad, beaming smiles. "What? No! You're showing us how to live dreams! We love you!" And I found myself in the middle of a 125-person group hug, the best hug of my life.

It turns out that when we have the courage to be vulnerable, ask for help, and speak our fears out loud to people, we open ourselves up to be flooded with joy and love, too.

Despite the group love fest, I still had an internal choice to make. I had to discern for myself which storyline I was going to hold, which narrative I would believe:

> *Option 1: Huge disappointment and a quitter; a total imposter*
> *—OR—*
> *Option 2: Inspiring role model for how to follow your dreams*

Months later, I got an email from the Lead Teacher, shortly before graduation. "I'm sure you're already busy and it's okay if you can't make it, I kept forgetting to tell you, but the students voted. They want you to be their Graduation Speaker." I cleared my calendar and showed up for the students I loved, who had shown up so beautifully for me.

I'm so glad I went with Option 2.

Challenging Times Are Opportunities for Practice

It's the year 2020 right now, the year we've learned new words and phrases: novel coronavirus-19; social distancing; Safer at Home; shelter in place. The pandemic has presented a perfect opportunity for me to come face-to-face with my old friend, Imposter Syndrome.

Wonderful! While I do not welcome the pandemic—which as of today, has no clear end in sight—I welcome the opportunity to continue putting the Touchstones into practice. The most challenging of times provides us with even more opportunity to apply the Touchstones in our lives. I welcome the plentiful reminders that this work of overcoming Imposter Syndrome isn't a "one and done" lesson that grants you immunity forever. It is *not* just like riding a bike. So you can just take that pressure off of yourself, right now. Overcoming your Imposter Syndrome is not a competition with an award for the Best Overcomer. No, it's just you, yourself, and your ego, doing the work with great love and compassion, consistently, over time.

However, the good news is that just like the aikido master in the story in the Introduction who has learned to recover his balance more quickly, one day we realize that we, too, have learned to find our balance more quickly. Like aikido practitioners who literally repeat a sequence thousands of times, the more we consciously use the Touchstones, the better we'll become at using them almost without thought—we will develop new habits.

I had my first pandemic opportunity to practice Interdependence when the major contract I had lined up for 2020 was rescinded, days before signing. The organization wanted to rethink their budget priorities in light of COVID-19. I completely understood their position intellectually, but emotionally, I felt what I thought was solid ground collapse under my feet.

But that's not what triggered my Imposter Syndrome. It was telling people that I lost work, especially other consultant friends and colleagues, especially those who were, in fact, still quite busy. Whoosh—childhood feelings welling up, big time. I felt like there was something wrong with me, that I wasn't being picked for the team. I heard the old voice say, "See? People always let you down. You can't depend on them for anything. No one cares, no one is here to help. You can't think your way out of this one, and you shouldn't have let this happen."

Sounds like a great head space to be in while going out to find new client work, doesn't it? It's like trying to get a date when you're desperately lonely—everything you do and say just oozes and drips with neediness. You might attract someone that way, but I guarantee it won't be who you wanted to attract.

So, I resisted my tendency to withdraw and hide my vulnerable feelings by remembering to Embrace Interdependence:

- I reminded myself that I'm not alone. In addition to my husband, I have a network of family, friends, and colleagues who care about my well-being, and who would want to know if I was struggling in some way.
- I reminded myself that if someone I cared about had this happen, I'd want them to call me so I could listen, offer support, and laugh or cry with them, as they needed.
- I talked with my husband and shared my business financial plan with him. Then together, we developed a solid family financial plan that eased my worries.
- I recalled all the times that I've been helped in the past and how people were happy to have the opportunity to show that they cared. They would see it as a compliment to be called, not as a burden.
- I reminded myself that despite what the headlines can lead us to believe, people are fundamentally good, kind, generous, and caring. I can trust others, and I can trust myself to know who to trust (see Discernment).

- I recognized that there were gifts in the situation—having time for long walks on a daily basis, my husband as a home officemate, and the mental and energetic capacity and time to write this book!

I'm so glad I remembered to reach out to my inner circle of trusted colleagues for support. I might still have worries or concerns, but I don't have to bear them alone or pretend everything's fine. When I ask for and receive help, I have the strength to fully accept my situation as it is, instead of wanting things to be different than they are. This acceptance frees up my energy to face the situation with more clarity and calm. Being in that kind of mental and emotional space is much more conducive to finding ways to work through challenges with confidence and creativity, and I'm also able to be a source of support and encouragement for others, too. When I'm not in a panic, I won't drag down the lifeguards who swim over to help me. We can swim to shore, together.

Each day I move toward that which I do not understand. The result is a continuous accidental learning which constantly shapes my life.
—Yo Ma

Isolation Feeds Imposter Syndrome

I have to say that, at first, it did not feel comfortable at all to admit some of my more insecure Imposter Syndrome thoughts to you. In fact, I started coming up with reasons to get up out of my chair and do just about anything except write this chapter. But you know what? As soon as I put my most private, insecure thoughts out there in the light of day, to be seen by you and everyone else who reads this book, I felt light and free.

As we've seen, Imposter Syndrome likes nothing more than a cold, dark, solid brick tower of isolation. When we step out of isolation and share our hearts with others, we free ourselves—and we are the only ones holding the tower's key. In my late twenties, I made a shocking discovery that flipped my worldview on its head. The discovery didn't come like a flash of lightning, in a moment of sudden epiphany. I crawled toward it inch by painful inch, taking many detours and winding up at dead end roads along the way.

Because of my shattered sense of security in childhood, I developed codependency, an unhealthy survival strategy that makes sense for navigating unpredictable, addicted, and mentally ill caretakers but doesn't work so well when you're trying to have healthy relationships outside of that situation. Codependence can be broadly defined as feeling overly concerned about and responsible for the feelings and actions of others, particularly loved ones. Imposter Syndrome and codependence are perfectly designed to cozy up together, since both rely on preoccupation with what other people are thinking about us and seeking approval for our worth outside of ourselves.

In my misguided attempts to be validated as okay, I twisted myself like a contortionist into whatever shape I thought would get approval and acceptance. Whatever I thought you wanted or needed me to be for you to like me, I did my best to accommodate. I tried to talk and dress like the people I hung out with and had no idea what my own style actually was. My first boyfriend loved Pink Floyd, so I'd sit and listen to "The Wall" for hours without saying, "Hey, can we listen to something else?" and putting on music I liked, which I was afraid was the wrong music to like. I became embarrassingly obsequious with people and had little sense of who I was, what I liked, what I wanted. I walked around feeling like an imposter—because I was.

I've already told you about how I developed a sense of extreme independence (no one cares, I have to take care of myself). I also became codependent—my self-worth relied on what others thought of me. The biggest danger of Imposter Syndrome is falling into either of these traps.

I fell into both, which resulted in me getting even further away from my goal, which was to love, be loved, and authentically connect. I woke up to what I was doing bit by bit. Therapy was helping, and so was watching Oprah, reading every self-help book I could find, and journaling—I became a self-improvement junkie. I was going to make myself better, damn it. I didn't realize that I was simply painting the walls and changing the artwork, when what I needed to do was heal a cracked foundation.

In the mid-2000's, I had the good fortune to go on a retreat at a place called Diana's Grove. Their tagline was, "If for you, imagining nature is not enough..." As a child who spent her days wandering woods and fields, this called to me. I showed up in the middle of nowhere in the Ozarks, a little freaked out after a long, twisting drive in the rain through the dense Mark Twain National Forest, nervously noting the Confederate flags hanging from trees along the almost deserted county roads. I emerged in a wonderland—a crystal clear creek running through wooded banks, rustic but beautiful cabins, outdoor private showers open to sun and sky, a seven-circuit labyrinth mown into a meadow filled with wildflowers. That week, in the company of strangers who became community, I let the people and natural environment fill me with the courage to break out of my cocoon. For a week, I was a butterfly.

You see, they didn't know a thing about me, and I didn't know them. I couldn't be who I thought they wanted me to be because those expectations—real or imagined—just didn't exist. I was... me. I laughed, danced, and sang. I got up and did a skit with another camper, and afterwards, someone came up and asked where I did my theater training. Who, me? Sad, scared, obsequious Jen was far away. I had seen my true nature behind the dark clouds. When the week ended, I vowed to become an integrated, whole self—to have the self I saw that week match the self I was in my everyday life. I decided to stop being an imposter.

I started doing small experiments. I started offering my real opinions. I started to have preferences for where I wanted to go to eat and say them out loud to my group of friends. I started to find my style, changing my hair and clothes to see what fit. And in the course of those experiments, I saw that people who started to get to know the authentic me liked me *more*, not less—the opposite of my fearful belief system that kept me isolated and contorted for so long.

Our True Nature is Interdependence

Being in healthy, authentic relationships and accepting the reality of true Interdependence will provide your heart and soul with nourishment and strength to overcome Imposter Syndrome. Remember, you don't have to do this all on your own, which goes against our true nature and our natural state of interdependence. The more we wake up to this reality, the more we resist isolation and Imposter Syndrome, the more we and everyone around us can grow, together.

> *In order to transform the world, we must transform ourselves.*
> —Grace Lee Boggs

Touchstone Practice: Embracing Interdependence

If you're struggling with seeking out and accepting help, being vulnerable and admitting your fears to others, admitting when you don't know or are uncertain, here are some practical steps you can take to shift unhealthy beliefs and habits that keep us isolated and fearful.

1. Get curious! Get out a journal and write down your thoughts and feelings. Then, go back and question your thoughts and beliefs. Ask yourself if there's another way to see the situation than the way you are seeing it currently.
2. Experiment with being truthful about a mistake instead of trying to cover it up or lie. If you are employed, try this with something small at work such as missing a typo in the report or turning something in a bit late. Instead of making excuses or getting defensive (two things that put us out of healthy relationship with others), take responsibility: "I'm sorry I missed that typo. Thank you for pointing that out to me," or "I had trouble getting my report in on time. I apologize for missing the deadline." Then observe what happens—are people more or less upset with you than if you offered excuses? Do you feel differently inside?
3. You may have heard the saying, "The problem is the solution." If you struggle with asking for help, then the solution is to do exactly that—ask for help. You can ask friends or family for help, or seek out a therapist or coach who can help you look at things in new light.
4. Try expressing your honest opinion instead of going along with someone else's, starting with a small thing, like deciding what to do with a friend. If your friend asks you to do something you don't really want to do, try saying, "Thank you for asking me. I really appreciate the invitation. I'm not really into that

particular activity, but how about going mini-golfing (or whatever you actually like) instead?"
5. Practice heart sharing. Sit down with someone you love and who loves you, and ask them if they'll just listen, without replying or giving advice or trying to "fix" anything. Ask that they keep everything you say confidential, and request that when you're done speaking, that they not bring up anything you said with you. Set a timer for three minutes, and without rehearsing, just speak from your heart. Begin with the words, "What is really in my heart is..." Allow yourself to say whatever rises up. Then, offer your loved one the same invitation and hold space for them to experience being heard, just as they did for you.
6. If you grew up in a home with trauma, abuse, or addiction, you may want to seek out groups such as ACOA (Adult Children of Alcoholics) or other Codependency Recovery groups.
7. Read books such as *How to Be an Adult* or *The Marriage Rules* to learn more about having healthy boundaries while in relationship with other people.

CHAPTER FOUR

Be Generous

Generous: marked by abundance; characterized by a noble or kindly spirit (Merriam-Webster)

When in your life have you been stunned by an unexpected gift? Cast back in your mind, looking for the sparkles of unbidden generosity that glisten like precious jewels strung along your life's timeline.

> *Steve showing up to help with all the literal big moves I've made, quietly and efficiently working without any expectation of thanks (and who I had to trick to pay for lunch).*

> *Sarah, who came to see me at the end of a terrible day, sitting in meditation with me and bestowing gifts of chocolate and the Magic Pants.*

> *Many friends rallying after I broke my collarbone while mountain biking—Coney bringing a TV (I didn't own one), an old VCR. and a stack of videos; Rhonda driving me to doctor's appointments; Susan offering to clean my house; Sam bringing me food and cleaning the wounds on my back that I couldn't reach.*

> *Ashlee and Aurora meeting me at the park to play on a gray fall day, surprising me with birthday cake and sunshine yellow flowers.*

My list could go on for a hundred pages, and I'd still not be able to recall or write about all the times I've been the recipient of generosity. I hope your list is just as long, full of gestures small and large that let us know we're seen, we matter, we're valued.

In my professional life, I would be nowhere without generosity. Every promotion, every new position, every client I've had came from a generous act on someone's part—sometimes obvious, and sometimes without my knowledge.

I've definitely been the recipient of ungenerous behavior as well. We all have. And, I would venture to say, we've all been the giver, too. It seems inevitable that as we fumble and stumble through hard passages and hard knocks, we will crash into others, step on toes, and cause others to stumble.

Pie People or Fish and Loaves People

Our brains are biologically primed to remember the hurts and store them away. This is a necessary survival instinct to keep ourselves from harm—don't eat that flower, be wary around that person, don't go near that submerged log near the riverbank. We scan our environments to quickly assess friend or foe, food or poison, safety or danger. Even with our beautifully evolved cerebral cortexes that allow us to write operas and books, build bridges and airplanes, lead movements and social revolutions, we still have the instinct to protect ourselves from pain and danger—real or perceived. Whether we let our defensive instincts rule our outlook and see wolves around every corner or we teach ourselves to see a world full of willing hands reaching to help us up and over any obstacle, that is up to us. It's also up to us to either clench our fists tightly or hold our hands open.

Simply put, I think we learn to be either "pie people" or "fish and loaves people" in our personal, professional, and social lives. We can be either one depending on circumstances and how we're feeling on any given day, but I think we tend to have learned one or the other that becomes our (often unconscious) primary default view of the world.

Pie people see the world of resources and opportunities as finite. There's only so much pie, and if you want a piece, you've got to get yours. Like Aunt Lucy's coveted pumpkin pie on the holiday dessert table, you may not get a piece if you don't elbow out your cousins and Uncle Larry. When it's gone, it's gone, and you either got some, or you didn't.

Fish and loaves people believe that there is enough for everyone, and, in fact, when there are more of us showing up, there will be even more to go around. This reference comes from a biblical passage where a crowd of 5,000 showed up. The disciples pulled Jesus aside in a secluded space and said they were going to send everyone away to find their own food because they only had five loaves and two fishes. Jesus instructed them not to turn people away, assuring them there would be plenty. He offered thanks and began breaking bread. Miraculously, everyone was fed and satisfied.

President Barack Obama understood interdependence on a national scale, and he caught a lot of heat and blowback for it. He gave a speech in 2012 about why we should continue to contribute tax dollars to support governmental infrastructure.

> *Look, if you've been successful, you didn't get there on your own. You didn't get there on your own. I'm always struck by people who think, well, it must be because I was just so smart. There are a lot of smart people out there. It must be because I worked*

> *harder than everybody else. Let me tell you something—there are a whole bunch of hardworking people out there.*
>
> *If you were successful, somebody along the line gave you some help. There was a great teacher somewhere in your life. Somebody helped to create this unbelievable American system that we have that allowed you to thrive. Somebody invested in roads and bridges. If you've got a business—you didn't build that. Somebody else made that happen. The Internet didn't get invented on its own. Government research created the Internet so that all the companies could make money off the Internet.*
>
> *The point is, is that when we succeed, we succeed because of our individual initiative, but also because we do things together.*

President Obama was, and still is, a fish and loaves kind of guy. He and First Lady Michelle Obama continue to give generously to individuals and communities through The Obama Foundation. When I was asked to volunteer my time and skills and serve as an Executive Coach in the Obama Fellows program, it was an easy yes. I want to be part of giving back to up-and-coming leaders who are working to create the kind of just, equitable, sustainable, and peaceful world that I want to live in. ¡Si se puede! Together, we can.

Debunking the Bootstrap Myth

In Chapter 2, I wrote about the false sense of fierce independence and "trust no one" attitude I'd cultivated. Part of what helped it take such deep hold is that It seemed to be working on multiple levels. I believed in the "bootstrap" mythology of the American dream and credited my own hard work for most of my success. My parents didn't pay for college. I worked full-time while I carried a full course load through four years of undergrad and two more years of grad school, with practicum and internships on top of that. Sounds like the classic "poor kid makes good" story, right?

Well, the reality is that I had a lot of help along the way, just not in the form of tuition payments. My oldest friend Dan grew up in the next town over and knew what it was like to have to pay your own way. His mom did her best, but she only had so much to give from her salary to help him go to school. We understood each other in a way that our more affluent friends never could. I was on the verge of having to drop out because my work-study job just wasn't enough to make ends meet. Dan had a car and a job at an art framing shop. He didn't have to, but he brought me in for an interview, got me hired, and drove me to work with him shift after shift. He never asked for thanks and brushed it off when I tried.

His generosity is part of my "self-made woman" story. I have dozens more examples about all the people who extended a hand when I was about to fall. The hands appeared, as I made my way, stepping stone by stepping stone, until I graduated. I wasn't too proud to reach back and grab them, and I can only hope that I've been that hand for others enough in my life to pay it all forward.

For much of my early life, I didn't act generously a lot of the time, especially when it came to money. I was terrified of not having any, given the turmoil and fear that filled the atmosphere in my home. It felt that we were always teetering on the brink of disaster, and that kind of unpredictable stress settled into my bones. I lived in a hypervigilant state of stress, always scanning for threats to any amount of security I managed to make for myself. I remember my partner at the time telling me that I didn't have to wear underwear with holes and convincing me that we had enough to buy new ones.

I had to learn to unclench my hands and relax. I had to learn that it's when we give that we receive. I can say with absolute conviction that I would not have a successful consulting business without the repeated generosity of many people throughout my network and by having a reputation for being generous as well. We all have different ways we can give, and I'm not only talking about money. We can give time, support, praise, information, meals, compliments, referrals, credit, recommendations—there are so many ways to be generous.

Generosity Begins at Home

I don't like to admit this, but one day not that long ago, I heard about a colleague's huge success in an endeavor, and my first reaction was jealousy—a sure hint that Imposter Syndrome is at play. Fortunately, I was in a space where I could slow down and get curious on the spot. Where the heck was this coming from? My colleague is someone I genuinely care about and like, and I want them to succeed and do well. Why was I feeling so ungenerous?

The more I sat and reflected on this event and on other times when I've felt jealous or not able to celebrate another's good fortune, the more I began to tune in to what was happening in me. I've come to call this being low resourced. When I have been struggling with my own self-confidence, feeling like I'm emotionally shaky, overwhelmed, overtired, or upset about a personal conflict—when there are things going on that I've let rattle me—I am less likely to be generous with myself, and therefore, it is very hard to be generous with others. We can't give to others what we can't, don't, or won't give to ourselves.

If I stay in this place of stinginess, I won't reach out and congratulate my colleague on her success. I might gossip about her or find another way to minimize her success: "You know, she only got that contract because her husband's best friend's tennis coach is on the Board." It's not pretty!

I invite you to reflect and think of a time when you reacted in a similarly petty way and found yourself tearing someone down—even someone you care about—instead of building them up, either directly or to others. I guarantee that there is no greater harm to your own reputation than to be known as someone who is mean-spirited and ungenerous.

Generosity is a Choice

I believe that if we were to dissect Imposter Syndrome down to its molecular material, all we'd find is just one thing—fear. When we're afraid, we get flooded with stress hormones that prepare us to respond efficiently to danger. In other words, we are not relaxed, open, mindful, or rational. I would also argue that we are not generous because our primary instinct is to save ourselves.

There are certainly exceptions, which is why we love stories about heroes (which I'm using as a gender-neutral word). Heroes are people, or other animals, who put themselves in peril to save others. When interviewed after the crisis is over, people will say things like, "I didn't even think about it," or "I just reacted. I'm not a hero." We tend to feel dissatisfied with these responses and even accuse them of false modesty, when I think they are being utterly honest. We want to believe that they made a heroic decision, because we desperately want to believe in heroes in our sometimes dangerous and scary world.

Generosity is a *conscious* choice. I certainly believe it can become a deeply ingrained habit and our default way of being to the point where it seems effortless and thoughtless. We see this in some people who are generous "without a second thought." But there *was* the first thought, even if it was so quick that we didn't observe it, to extend themselves on another's behalf. When people develop the habit of choosing generosity, then it appears to be second nature.

Generosity Is Relational, Not Transactional

Hopefully, you're beginning to see just how interwoven each of the Ten Touchstones in this book are. They are interdependent, and speaking of which... If we haven't learned to Embrace Interdependence, then it's going to be difficult for us to be generous for generosity's sake, not because of what we think we might get in exchange.

So why bother to cultivate a generous nature? It's not required to "make it" by our U.S. capitalist culture's standards. We have phrases for it, like "she clawed her way to the top" or "they stepped on a lot of heads to get there" or "he probably sold his firstborn for that promotion." While some people may cringe, a lot of people applaud and celebrate the person who beats everyone out. Look at "Shark Tank."

Generosity is all about honoring ourselves and others. How I act toward you is one and the same thing as how I act toward myself. If I am mean-spirited and begrudging with you, then you can bet that I am having mean-spirited and begrudging thoughts about myself. In this sense, every action is *relational*, a cycle of exchange that flows between me, you, and all the world.

When we forget this essential truth, we may approach our relationships and our interdependent *interactions* with others as if they were *transactions*. Transactions have their place. When I hand someone $3.00 at my local coffee shop, I hope they hand a coffee back to me.

However, if I volunteer myself for a favor and then keep score in my mind, waiting for the other person to reciprocate, then I've turned what appeared to be a *relational* and generous act into a *transaction*—I want my coffee, so to speak, and I'll remember you owe me one.

This has a harmful effect on our relationships. Even if we never say a word, we will communicate what is in our hearts. Humans exude an emotional field that extends beyond our bodies. We communicate volumes with the slightest tone, with just a subtle head tilt, with a miniscule flicker of tension around our eyes. We are equally good at reading these energetic and physical cues, and "you owe me" takes the shine of goodwill off of the "gift" we received. What we thought was the extended hand of generosity remains extended, waiting for us to put something back in it.

We can guard against this keeping of accounts by getting clear with ourselves *before* we give. It's okay to do a trade. My friend Lizza and I work-trade frequently. We trade edits on documents, coaching on sticky issues, and facilitation strategies. But we're clear about what we're doing, and we agree on the terms from the start. There are other times when we're just being generous and giving gifts in the spirit of loving friendship, and we're clear about that, too. Both feel clean, because we're clear.

So get really clean and clear in your heart and mind before you give. Is the gift really a gift, free and clear of any obligation? Do you have an expectation of reciprocity? Do you expect an expression of appreciation?

For those of us recovering from codependency and/or Imposter Syndrome, that last one is a real kicker. We, more than others, deeply want to feel appreciated. To be clear, I think appreciation is something that we all consistently underestimate and under-give. I've done many organizational culture assessments, and I have yet to see one that didn't have in its findings that people want "more appreciation and recognition from management." In fact, I remember reading about a study that found that more people would rather get more recognition and praise from their supervisor than get more money in their paycheck.

Giving to Get Is Not Generosity

What we're talking about here is motivation. If I do something *in order to* get praise, then we've just created a pretty icky (to use a highly sophisticated and technical term) relationship with the person we're supposedly helping. We get into trouble when we act in transactional ways with people with whom we are trying to cultivate relationships, particularly when we're trying to establish trust.

For example, a person I considered to be a close friend sent an email out to a bunch of people one day stating that she only had so much time and energy to give, and she'd decided to pursue friendships with a chosen few. Sorry, you didn't make the cut, I wish you well, have a good life. I believe that it sounded way better in her head and that she thought she was setting healthy boundaries, but whoa—it was tone deaf and shocking to be on the receiving end of that email.

Several years later, I looked at my ringing phone and saw she was on the line. "Interesting," I thought, and I took the call to see what she had to say, keeping an open mind and door. After several minutes of conversation in which she asked how I'd been, showed interest in my well-being, and told me she missed me, there it came—she wanted me to volunteer my time and give money to her political campaign. Ewww. Icky. This is a really good example of someone being transactional (reducing friendship to time and energy given, then asking for time and money back in exchange for a few minutes of niceties) rather than relational. There was no trust or authentic relationship being offered or developed in either exchange, as evidenced by the fact that after I thanked her and gently declined to give my time and money (I was already supporting another candidate), I never heard from her again.

When we conduct our professional relationships in a transactional way rather than in a relational way, we leave ourselves susceptible to Imposter Syndrome because, as we've seen in other examples, we are actually being imposters. She called me up *acting* like someone who cared about me as a person, but not truly *being* caring toward me as a person.

The best way to not feel icky and inauthentic is through generosity—to be caring, kind, considerate, supportive, compassionate, and helpful to people for the sake of being in right relationship with them, not to get something we want from them—even a thank you.

Cultivating the Habit of Generosity

Try this out for yourself. Begin to notice when you have the thought, "Jeez, he could have said thanks." Stop immediately and get curious—what am I thinking and feeling right now? Am I feeling insecure about something? Is there something I want or need that I'm not getting? We can usually find the source of our ungenerous thoughts and desire for praise if we sit quietly and ask ourselves questions that we have the courage to answer honestly.

Conversely, begin to observe all the ways people are generous with you throughout your day. Did the UPS driver hold the door for you on her way out of the lobby? Did Mariella pay you a compliment in front of the whole Leadership Team? Did the clerk at the grocery store compliment your glasses? Did your boss tell you how impressed she was with your contributions on the project? Examples of generosity that flow our way abound if we look for them.

Noticing the ways other people are being generous with us helps us fill our own generosity well, shoring us up against "low resource" days when we're not feeling like our best selves. Instead of faking like we're good people and being imposters, we can remember that we have a deep well of generosity that has been filled by others. From this well of abundance, we can pour some out for those around us, filling our own glass first.

The Power of Generosity to Change the World

One of the most moving examples of generosity in the face of atrocity that I've heard comes from the stories told by President Nelson Mandela and other Freedom Fighters in the anti-apartheid movement who were imprisoned in dehumanizing conditions on Robben Island off the coast of Cape Town, South Africa. I've been there and heard the stories firsthand, as all of the guides at Robben Island were formerly imprisoned there.

In a place where it would be all too easy to look out for yourself, or give in to despair, or to lose your spirit and very humanity, the men shored each other up through acts of generosity. To cultivate infighting, the guards devised a system of distributing food according to race. The men responded by sharing their differently-sized meal portions and dividing it equally, among everyone. Each new prisoner was given a political education and taught by those who had been there longer, and they were expected to teach another in turn. Their motto was, "Each one, teach one."

Imagine if we all took this generosity of spirit into our own lives, workplaces, and communities and truly became our brothers' and sisters' keepers. There would be no room for imposters in such a world, for we would have no fear of each other.

Touchstone Practice: Be Generous

A wonderful way to practice cultivating a spirit of authentic generosity is through a combination of observation, inquiry, and noticing. Here is a recap of the steps I wrote about in the previous section to try out for yourself:

1. Observe: Notice when you're feeling resentful toward someone for not appreciating or thanking you in the way you think they should.
2. Inquire: What am I thinking and feeling right now? Am I feeling insecure about something? Is there something I want or need that I'm not getting?
3. Notice: Gather evidence of generosity all around you. Did the UPS driver hold the door for you on her way out of the lobby door? Did your coworker pay you a compliment in front of the whole team? Did the clerk at the grocery store compliment your glasses? Did your boss tell you how impressed she was with your contributions on the project?

CHAPTER FIVE

Learn to Heal

"Someone was hurt before you, wronged before you, hungry before you, frightened before you, beaten before you, humiliated before you, raped before you... yet, someone survived. You can do anything you choose to do."
—Dr. Maya Angelou

Healing our core wounds takes time, attention, and care. It is a process, not a quick fix. It might hurt more before it gets better, like anyone who has ever had wound or burn debridement knows. Removing what is dead or damaged in our hearts and minds to make way for what is healed and healthy can hurt like hell—but if we don't do it, we are guaranteed to suffer and not be fully alive and well.

You've probably heard people say, "Life is not for the faint of heart," or "Life isn't for wimps," or simply, "Life is hard." I don't think there's a soul among us who gets through unscathed. I also don't think there's much value in comparing hurts to see if our own hurts are worthy of suffering. If we hurt, we hurt—someone else's pain doesn't invalidate our own, even if theirs seems more extreme.

What matters most is that we recognize that when we heal ourselves, we help others heal. You may have heard the expression, "Hurt people, hurt people." Our unhealed wounds cause us to talk and act and think in ways that hold us back from our full potential, and we affect everyone around us as well. You may have heard it stated this way: the boss yells at the employee, the employee goes home and yells at her husband, her husband yells at the child, and the child kicks the dog. In my home, this was literally true, only the boss wasn't required, and we kids didn't kick the dog, but each other. The details may differ, but it illustrates how wounded folks pass on their hurt, often taking it out on those with less power, so the innocent get wounded.

If we didn't have wounds, it would be highly unlikely that we'd have Imposter Syndrome. The good news is that we can overcome Imposter Syndrome even if our wounds are in various stages of healing—the key is recognizing that our wounds exist and tending them with compassionate care until they close rather than continuing to bleed all over us and everyone around.

> *"The function of freedom is to free someone else."* Toni Morrison
>
> It's June 2020, and communities all over the U.S. and the world are marching, demanding justice and systemic change to stop the terrorism and killing of Black and brown people. My white brothers and sisters are waking up, realizing the privilege they have of mostly ignoring what people of color can't ignore for one minute, even inside their homes.
>
> I do not walk in the world in black or brown skin, and I have said to people of color, thinking I was being a good white ally, "I can't ever know what you feel." One of my teachers, Dr. Alana Tappin, has the view that this only further separates us from each other, which is already one of the toxic consequences of

racism. She says to white people that you may not be black or brown, but you do know what it feels like to be in pain. You have felt what injustice feels like. You have had your share of grief and sorrow. You've likely felt afraid of bodily harm at least once in your life. You can understand, and through your understanding, feel the kind of empathy that impels you to do something.

Learning about the impact a racist society has on all of us and working together to be actively anti-racist is part of our healing work to counter Imposter Syndrome. I think those of us who are white get that no matter how poor or tough our early lives were, we have advantages simply because of our skin color and membership in the dominant culture. For centuries, we have been taught that whiteness is superior to blackness. For centuries, the very laws of this land have enforced and ensured separateness and advantage. Why wouldn't we feel, in our bodies and hearts and minds, that our seats at the table were, at least in part, granted to us through no effort of our own? That thought makes many people uneasy and defensive.

When we can name and acknowledge this, we can begin to heal. We can learn to undo the biases we've internalized that stem from the message that black is bad, white is good. Everyone, people of color included, have been fed this poisonous mental construct since childhood. You can find numerous podcasts, readings, and videos online to continue your self-education about how this toxic state of being came to be—which was by design, by the white male elite, for their own economic gain.

> I hope my white brothers and sisters, me included, keep waking up to all the ways that racism hurts all people, including those complicit with oppression as well as the oppressed. I hope we stop sleepwalking and take anti-racist action for longer than one news cycle about George Floyd's murder and keep up the work for as long as it takes.

Heal Your Story, Heal Yourself

So how do we heal? Well, I can't actually tell you exactly how to heal yourself, but I *can* tell you about ways that have worked for others, and I can tell you what healing has looked like for me. As life coach Martha Beck said, after observing wildlife on safari, "You can't pull a buffalo from the mud; it has to climb out under its own steam. When you can pull yourself out of your own muck, by giving your same old stories happier endings, you'll find that rage turns to peace, pain to power, fear to courage."

I deeply believe that in order to heal, we have to heal our stories, because we literally create our entire world with them. Imposter Syndrome is a thing only—and I do mean only—because of the stories we tell ourselves.

Hold up a minute, you might be thinking. Reality is real. I don't make things up. I invite you to try this idea on and see if it just might be true. You can return to your way of thinking if you don't agree, I promise.

One of my favorite quotes comes from Viktor Frankl, an Austrian neurologist and psychiatrist who survived unimaginable horrors during the Holocaust. He wrote, "Between stimulus and response there is a space. In that space is our power to choose our response. In our response lies our growth and our freedom."

The Three Levels of Reality

Let's take a closer look at the space between stimulus and response where our freedom and healing can be found. I'm going to share a model with you that literally changed my life and immediately began to help me improve all of my relationships in my personal and professional lives, and most importantly, with myself.

This model has its roots in almost every tradition there ever was, in every myth and fable and story ever told, and in many of the major schools of philosophy ever devised. The idea that reality is created by our perception is not a new one. I call it The Three Levels of Reality, and it's a slightly modified version of the model I learned from my mentors, Cynthea Jones and Patricia Storm (who slightly modified the original model taught to them by their mentor, Jean Houston).

Level One—Physical Reality

This is the world of tangible phenomenon, things that we can perceive through our senses of sight, touch, hearing, taste, and smell. As we know from research, our human senses are limited in scope, so there is much of the world we don't perceive (like colors in the spectrum or sounds our ears and brains can't register but are perfectly clear to dogs), but we're talking about our human experience, so it works for this model.

Examples of physical reality are things like: I smell lilacs and orange blossoms in the bouquet on my desk; I'm typing on a keyboard; I'm sitting on a stool that is 23" tall.

This is the level of reality we think we live in all the time. Our bodies do, but our minds? Very rarely.

Level Two—Mythic Reality

Welcome to the Land of Story, the true home of the mind and our ego. When I'm teaching this model in workshops, at this point I ask folks to raise their hands if they think they are creative. As you might imagine, only a few folks raise their hands. Would you? You and everyone in every room should have both hands up, way up. All of us are wildly creative because we are making things up all day long, and on top of that, we believe our stories to be true.

Here's how it works.

Imagine that in physical reality, you're in a meeting, and you share an idea. Across the table, you see David roll his eyes.

Quick as lightning, you have a thought about David rolling his eyes. Here are some popular thoughts one can have when someone rolls their eyes after we speak in a meeting:

- Oh crap, I've upset David.
- There goes David again, disrespecting me and my ideas.
- Jeez, can't you even give my idea a little consideration?
- *Fill in what you would think—or have thought—in this situation.*

It happens so very fast, so fast that we're hardly aware of the space between the event (stimulus) and our reaction (response). And then because most of the time, we believe our thought to be true, we are led into...

Level Three—Emotional Reality

Welcome to the Land of Feelings, ruled by the Land of Story, loosely based on Physical Reality.

Our emotions respond to our thoughts. This is why the movies work. We know that Harry Potter survives being attacked by "He Who Shall Not Be Named," because we know there are several more books in which he is very much alive, but even so, we feel fear and anxiety—Harry's in danger!

The thought, "Harry's in danger!" creates an emotional reality of anxiety and fear. Emotions are physiological reactions. What we label "afraid" is a collection of sensations: accelerated heart rate, sweaty palms, tense muscles, dilated pupils, rapid respiration. The truly fascinating thing is that we have this response *even though we know* Harry not only doesn't die, he isn't even real—he's pure fiction.

How Will You Direct the Scene?

Going back to our meeting example, the thought, "Why does David think my idea sucks?" is also a fiction. When we think it, we are likely to have an emotional reaction. Some emotions we might feel are ashamed, embarrassed, angry, despondent, sad, or a host of other emotions, maybe in combination.

When we think the thought and feel the feelings, then how might we react? And how do we get out of this drama in which we are the writer, producer, director, and star?

The only way I know is to slow down, get curious, and question "reality." When we've done the work to heal our wounds, we are far more able to do this than when we're operating from our hurt places.

The previous list I provided was a list of thoughts that Imposter Syndrome would write. When we are in a healthy, centered, and confident state, we'd likely have a distinctly different list:

- Is David okay?

- Hmmm, I value David's opinion—what might I be missing?
- Ah, David—I know he usually doesn't warm up to ideas quickly. He just needs some time with this.

These thoughts are no more real than the other list of thoughts, but you can feel the difference. The first list of thoughts cues us to be defensive, fearful, or angry—and when we're triggered into those emotions, our brains are flooded with stress hormones that keep us from being wise, resourceful, calm, and skillful. We react rather than respond, which is another way of saying that we give up our freedom to choose.

This list of thoughts is more likely to cue us to remain curious, open, and empathetic. These are feelings that increase the odds that we'll stay calm *and not take it personally.* We are far more likely to remember that we don't have the whole story or know what is going on with someone else, which is essential for maintaining healthy and emotionally intelligent relationships.

As Director of our own movie, let's yell, "Cut!" and retake the scene of the meeting with David

Take #2:

You've just shared your idea, and you see David roll his eyes (Physical Reality).

You slow down, reflect a moment, then say, "David, I noticed you rolled your eyes. Can you tell me what's up?" Or you could say, "David, I saw you roll your eyes, and my story is that you didn't like my idea. Is that true?" (questioning your Mythic Reality)

David says, "Sorry, I just saw a text from my daughter. She forgot to tell me that she has to bring 40 cupcakes for Snack Day tomorrow, and we're going to be at her brother's swim meet all evening. Argh!" (getting more information about David's Physical Reality, which shifts your Mythic Reality)

You say, "Oh my gosh, I hate when that happens!" with lots of sympathy, and the meeting rolls on (creating your Emotional Reality)

This, by the way, is a true story from one of my clients. She was off the chain mad but calmed herself and remembered the Three Levels of Reality. When she asked him about his eye roll, this is really what he said. She was relieved that she averted an epic misunderstanding.

Just for fun, let's go back to the meeting and play it out again, only this time you react out of a defensive story instead of responding with skill.

Take #3:

You've just shared your idea, and you see David roll his eyes (Physical Reality).

You don't ask David what that was about, and you believe the thought, "Guess David thinks my idea sucks!" (unquestioned Mythic Reality)

You experience a combination of anger and embarrassment. You begin avoiding eye contact with David, and when you do meet his gaze, your eyes and face give off subtle cues about your emotional state even though you're trying not to show how pissed off you are. (deep in your Emotional Reality)

Remember that David is also writing, directing, and starring in the drama of his world. He sees that something is off when you look at him, so he thinks and believes the thought that you are mad (and in this case, he is right!), but he has no idea why. If David is prone to Imposter Syndrome, it could kick in right about now. For example, he might think "I shouldn't even be in this meeting," and he might go silent, further compounding the weird and tense vibe in the meeting.

And all that happened in Physical Reality is… cupcakes.

You can see how easily, quickly, and frequently this plays out, day after day, in office after office. It's a wonder we get along at all! And it's also why we have an incredible opportunity to heal others when we heal ourselves. We literally have the freedom to choose to stop the chain reaction of ill will and negative thoughts that rubs salt in others' core wounds.

Taking 100% Responsibility for Our Healing

When we believe that other people are responsible for how we feel, we hand them the keys to our minds and hearts. When we take 100% responsibility for how we feel, no matter what happens we can, like the aikido master, recover our balance quickly.

Alice Walker wrote, "Healing begins where the wound was made." When we recognize that the place of wounding lies in what we think and believe about what happens to us, we are liberated. We discover that nothing and no one can take away our power to Learn to Heal.

Touchstone Practice: Learn to Heal

As with many of the other Touchstones, our sources of help with this Touchstone are the same: therapy, coaching, meditation, self-study. I find Byron Katie's *The Work* particularly helpful, which is a process for questioning our thoughts and beliefs. She teaches that the *only* source of suffering is what we're thinking and believing, and that we can live in either a state of war or a state of peace with our own minds. This exercise is based on her work.

Step One: Bring to mind a time when you felt the grip of Imposter Syndrome. Really go there—fill in all the details that you can: what you were wearing, the color of paint on the walls of the room, if you were drinking coffee or water, what the air smelled like. Relive it in your mind, as fully as you can.

Really slow down, get still, and listen—what thoughts were you having? Write them down on paper. When you get them on paper, you can see them and work with them.

Here's my list as an example:

- I am clueless—I have no idea what the heck to do next.
- They're totally going to find out that they hired the wrong person for this project.
- I can't tell them that I don't know what to do—they won't respect or trust me.
- You know who would know what to do? [Insert name of any other consultant I respect] would know what to do.
- Oh my god. I am never going to take on a project like this again.
- I can't stand this.

Step Two: One at a time, rewrite the thought as its opposite and see if you can find the truth in it. What evidence do you have that this new thought might be true?

Here's the important thing: whether it's true or not *does not matter* because our thoughts are *all* made up. What matters is how we think, feel, and act when we believe the thoughts we're having.

Imposter Syndrome Thoughts	**Empowering Thoughts**
I am clueless—I have no idea what the heck to do next.	I am not clueless—I have an idea of what to do next.
They're totally going to find out that they hired the wrong person for this project.	They're going to find out that they hired the right person for this project.
I can't tell them that I don't know what to do—they won't respect and trust me.	I can tell them that I don't know what to do—they will respect and trust me.
You know who would know what to do? [Insert name of any other consultant I respect] would know what to do. They should have hired them, not me.	You know who also might not know what to do? [Insert name of any other consultant I respect] might not know what to do.
Oh my god. I am never going to take on a project like this again.	Oh my god. I am definitely going to take on a project like this again.
I can't stand this.	I can stand this.

Step Three: Ask yourself: which set of thoughts keeps you in a calm, curious, open, and skillful mental and emotional state of being? Which set of thoughts make you more able to be of service to your clients, team, or manager?

By the way, when we Learn to Heal from Imposter Syndrome in our career, volunteer, or academic lives, we enjoy the wonderful side effect of becoming more skillful in all our personal relationships as well.

CHAPTER SIX

Just Surrender

How did the rose ever open its heart and give to this world all of its beauty? It felt the encouragement of Light against its being; otherwise we all remain too frightened.
—*Hafiz*

Many of my coaching clients show up with some variation of the same wish: I want to make a change, but I want to know how it's going to turn out before I make it. In other words, they want to make the *right* choice—the one that will turn out well and make life better.

There's nothing wrong with that, except that it's impossible. In twenty years as a coach and 51 years of living, I have seen how the deep-rooted desire for control limits our lives, keeps us playing small, and creates suffering for ourselves and those around us.

Imposter Syndrome and Perfectionism

There is a strong relationship between Imposter Syndrome and perfectionism. Psychologists have ongoing debates over perfectionism—what causes it, what mitigates it, what makes it adaptive or maladaptive, who is likely to develop it and why. For our purposes here, let's define perfectionism as setting unreasonably high expectations for yourself and then being intensely self-critical when you fail to achieve them.

Imposter Syndrome relies on comparison—we compare ourselves to others and find ourselves lacking. When we add perfectionism to the mix, we're throwing gasoline on the fire of our self-criticism.

What's tricky is that the world rewards perfection. Think about an Olympic-level figure skater, for example. She gets up at 4 am and devotes hours and hours of her life to her sport, on the ice, in the gym, in the dance studio, all in pursuit of the elusive perfect 10 and Olympic gold.

The pursuit of perfection in and of itself isn't inherently bad. A skater who finds joy in the striving and delights in the process of perfecting her routine at 5 am when no one is watching can thrive even under pressure of competition. She knows that she's skated a perfect program many times in her training, and she does her best to reproduce that performance when all eyes are on her, under the scrutiny of judges. She has done her best to prepare and then when she skates out to the center of the ice, she surrenders—to the music, to her muscle memory, to the pure joy of skating—and lets herself flow.

Let's consider another skater. She gets up at 4 am and pushes herself, bearing down and grinding away at her workouts, practice sessions, and time with her coach on the ice. When she's having an off day and is struggling to get her landings right, she becomes a storm cloud of anger and hears her coach's helpful suggestions as criticisms, painfully pointing out how far she is from doing it right. When she skates out into the center and waits for her music to start—she clenches and wills herself to be perfect this time. Sometimes she is. But when she's not, she falls apart and questions if she should even be in the sport anymore, even though deep down inside, she loves it. She looks at the winners on the podium with jealousy instead of admiration, and beats herself up for failing to win.

There is a difference between striving to perfect your craft and performance and striving to be perfect.

There's one more skater we haven't talked about. She doesn't even know she's a skater because she's never tried to be one. Ever since she was a kid, she was glued to the television whenever a skating competition was on. She loves the music, the costumes, the artistry, the athleticism of it all. But every time someone says, "Hey, why don't you try it?" she shakes her head and says, "No, that's okay. I don't think I'd be very good at that." She's never laced up and stepped out on the ice. She's never risked finding out she's right and can't skate well, but she's never allowed herself the joy of the experience at all.

Perfectionism can lead us to limit our world to the circle of what we know we're good at, so we never have to experience failure, and failure is something Imposter Syndrome can't tolerate.

Risk Failure, or Risk Regret

> *Twenty years from now you will be more disappointed by the things you didn't do than by the ones you did. So throw off the bowlines. Sail away from the safe harbor. Catch the trade winds in your sails. Explore. Dream. Discover.*
> —*Mark Twain*

The most important reason to make friends with the idea of not being in control and risking failure is so we can live fully, without denying ourselves the joy of discovering the abundance of experiences life has to offer.

Many years ago, I was hiking at Red Rock Canyon in Nevada, watching the rock climbers. I remember thinking how badass and cool they seemed, but never once considered that I could do that myself. I didn't and couldn't see myself as a climber. You can imagine how satisfying it was and how triumphant I felt when ten years later, I roped up and climbed on the very wall I'd wistfully hiked by in the past.

In my life, I've said "Yes!" to many adventures. I've kayaked in Antarctic sea ice, lived and worked on a lumber ship in Norway, backpacked and lived in the Rocky Mountains for a month, traveled solo in South America and South Africa, and plunged into standing waves on roiling rivers.

Imposter Syndrome and perfectionism show up more subtly in our daily lives and work. For me, it's no big deal to go up a rock face and try climbing a route that I likely won't be able to climb perfectly the first time, but I can feel mortal terror at the thought of bombing when facilitating a staff retreat. I am far more afraid of losing my clients' respect and confidence in me.

Playing It Safe

There have been plenty of times when I held myself back and missed opportunities, or would have if someone wasn't there to say, "You can do it." Sometimes that person was me.

When I let this fear get the better of me—when my Imposter Syndrome kicks in—I can get so caught up in protecting myself that I can lose sight of what matters most, compromise my own values, and harm my relationships with others. I can act and speak in ways that actually turn me into an imposter rather than being an authentic person who, like everyone else, makes mistakes and isn't perfect. When Imposter Syndrome has me in its grip, I can twist myself into knots to keep others from seeing the parts of me that I want to hide.

When I enter this place of trying to control others' perceptions and control how things turn out, I'm in the opposite state of surrender, of letting things unfold and trusting myself to respond to whatever happens.

Recently, I was leading a meeting with a team of educators. We had a loose agenda for our meeting, but part of the plan was to see what emerged from the team once we started to talk with each other. The meeting went in a direction that no one anticipated, and they ended up having an emotional conversation about trust and clearing up some assumptions and misunderstandings.

Afterwards, one of the team members asked me, essentially, how I could be okay with coming in without a clear plan and allowing a process to unfold. She was seeking to understand how to let go and trust. There is beauty in surrender, in remembering that even when we have agendas, we can't possibly control how things will actually go. When we let go and stop trying so hard to control, we create opportunities for ourselves and others to be authentic and real with each other.

I could easily relate to her question because I know what it feels like to *not* surrender and trust. Letting go and flowing is not something that came easily to me in the past, and I still struggle with it at times. I have a story that illustrates how hard I used to try to be perfect and in control—a story that could have turned out very differently if I didn't surrender.

Truth and Consequences

For a brief period of time, I was a traditional guidance counselor at a large comprehensive high school. I was responsible for students with last names beginning with S-Z, around 500 of them. One of my main jobs was to help them plan their schedules so they would graduate on time and be prepared to apply for college if they chose to do so. I carefully pored over my student files, reviewing to make sure everything was in order, especially as students neared graduation. One day, a senior stopped me in the hall and asked me if he needed one of his English classes for graduation. I answered that technically no, that he'd still graduate if he failed it.

Flash forward to the last few weeks of the semester, the second period of time in each semester when we sent failure notices home to students and parents to warn them that they were at risk of failing a class. As I reviewed his file and prepared his failure notice, I felt my body flood with an icy chill of realization—he actually did need that class to graduate.

I started beating myself up for my mistake, one that I couldn't take back or fix. I contemplated my options. I actually considered forging a copy of a letter to prove that I tried to warn him and his parents that he needed the class, to cover my tracks and put the blame somewhere else. I was so desperate in those days to be perfect and win others' approval that I couldn't stomach the thought that I'd made a huge mistake. I also failed to see the student's role and responsibility in the situation for tracking his own progress and the choice he made to skip the entire semester. I put the whole blame on me, and I was in a panic.

Our Guidance Director had extremely high standards, and we often disappointed her, which she let us know. She was also generous with praise when we met her standards, and as you know from what I've told you about my background, I spent my whole life seeking praise and approval. It hooked me like nothing else, which is why making a huge mistake could literally make me feel like everything was on the line. My safety, security, esteem, and belonging were all wrapped up in Being Good.

As I sat at my desk thinking of how to lie, freaking the hell out, I realized that even though I wanted nothing more than to escape the situation, I couldn't fix this. I needed help.

With a pit in my stomach, I went to the Guidance Director and confessed, readying myself for her judgement.

She surprised me completely when she said, "Thank you for telling me. No one is perfect, and I know how conscientious you are. We all make mistakes, and it happens when we have so many students. You shouldn't have told him that he didn't need the class in the hallway, but I can see how that happened. Let's figure out what to do." I was so relieved, and so glad that I didn't hurt myself by lying and creating even more guilt and suffering for myself, the young man, and his parents.

Unfortunately, the student didn't react with any grace— he was pissed off and glared at me whenever he saw me— but I could take just about anything from teens, and he did graduate, so that was okay. But I've never forgotten how I felt in that moment, and how I felt when I surrendered and stopped trying to control the situation to keep from looking and feeling like an imposter and a failure. In fact, I earned my Director's trust and approval even more because I had the courage to take responsibility for my actions. She could forgive a mistake, but she would not have forgiven a lie.

Even if she had gotten mad, she still would have helped me to solve the problem, which was the most important thing in the scenario. That's the other part of letting perfectionism blind us—we get so focused on keeping ourselves from experiencing painful feelings that we lose sight of our impact on others. I was willing to hurt a student and his family with a fake letter rather than feel like a failure. If I had done that, then I really would have been an imposter. I would not have been who I professed to be, which is a caring, committed counselor who believed in serving and supporting students to be their best.

Giving Ourselves Grace

The things we do and say out of fear of not being perfect, fear of failing, or fear of making mistakes can lead us to the very outcome we're trying so hard to avoid—we end up actually being fake instead of being honest, authentic, fallible people who do their best. So what can we do when we feel ourselves tied in knots of perfectionism, and we wistfully long to be free-flowing and unbound?

The first step is realizing and admitting that our thinking is causing problems for us. We can look for signs that we've gone beyond normal jitters and nerves about wanting to do well in our work to a state that is having a real and negative impact on our lives or those around us. Some of those signs can include:

- Engaging in hateful or demeaning self-talk
- Noticing that others are walking on eggshells or avoiding interactions with us
- Having emotional reactions that are out of control or disproportionate to relatively minor mistakes or incidents
- Harshly judging others for their mistakes or errors (e.g. projecting)

On a recent episode of Queer Eye (If you haven't watched the Fab Five in action, I strongly recommend you do!), a pastor confided in two of his peers that he felt shame for not coming out as gay earlier in life. Just before his confession, he'd shared a story about one of his parishioners who recently came out to his family as a young man, although his mother and grandmother were fairly certain that he was gay since he was four years old. One of the pastors said, "Would you ever tell that young man that he should have come out sooner?" He replied instantly, "No!" The pastor gently asked, "So why do you tell yourself that, child of God?" His eyes welled up and he cried as he whispered, "Thank you." In that moment, he realized that the grace he freely offers to others is the same grace he also deserves.

Touchstone Practice: Just Surrender

We can begin to loosen the knots in our thinking by being really curious and questioning our thoughts. Just as we learned in Chapter 5: Learn to Heal, we can see if there's more space and room in our thinking than we are allowing ourselves. It can be helpful to imagine what we would say to a dear friend who came to us with the same fears. As we look bravely and honestly at ourselves, it's essential to offer ourselves the same compassion and grace that we'd offer to anyone else we love.

Exercise:

1. Bring to mind a critical thought you have about yourself. Some clues that this is a critical thought is that you're using harsh or judgmental language with yourself that you would not use with someone you cared about, or out loud with anyone, for that matter. Without trying to clean it up or change it to sound less harsh, write down exactly what you say to yourself in your mind.
2. Now, imagine that someone you care about deeply is sitting in front of you. They say, "I want to tell you a thought I have about myself. I think (insert your thought in your exact words)."
3. Imagine what you might say to them. Write down your response or say it out loud.

4. Now, look at yourself in the mirror. Read or repeat your response to yourself while looking yourself in the eye with all the compassion and love you have for the person you just imagined in front of you. You may wish to place your hand over your heart to remind yourself to speak from a place of love and compassion.

CHAPTER SEVEN

Be Brave and Courageous

One isn't born courageous, one becomes it.
—Marjane Satrapi

The large staff returned to the meeting hall after the lunch break at their off-site retreat. Tensions had been brewing and there was a charge in the room. The senior leader sitting next to me squared her shoulders, took a deep breath, and took the microphone that I handed to her with an encouraging smile. I watched and listened as she spoke with passion, warmth, and sincerity. As she finished speaking, the staff began cheering and applauding enthusiastically, buoyed by her words. She dropped back down next to me with a sigh of relief and turned to me, eyes wide. I met her gaze and said with all the warmth I could convey, "That was courageous—well done!" She smiled a little and said, "No, it wasn't. I was scared the whole time."

When I debriefed with her and the rest of the planning team later, I asked her to go back to that moment. I wanted her, and the whole team who had put themselves on the line in service of bringing unity to a divisive situation, to see that she had actually been the very definition of courage, which is being afraid and taking action anyway. As she took in my words, I saw her whole body and energy shift—she sat up straighter and the tension left her face. Her perspective changed, and she became courageous in her own eyes.

The courage required to overcome Imposter Syndrome is not always visible to the room. There likely won't be cheering and applause because no one may realize your internal effort. But the wise, quiet observer within us, that which is our true nature, will see and know.

No Ego, No Imposter Syndrome

Philosophers, theologians, psychologists, mystics—over the centuries, humans have always asked, "Who am I?" Who is it who is reading this book, thinking these thoughts? Who goes out and interacts with the world, works at a job, plays with the kids, mows the lawn, and buys the groceries? Who is thinking? Who is this voice in my head, and who is listening?

Through my own experiences in therapy and meditation, I subscribe to the idea that we have an ego that is made up of our thoughts, and we believe that this ego is the real "me." The ego's job is to protect us from pain and seek what feels good, and our ego is so very convincing that we buy it hook, line, and sinker. We mistake our fragile ego for who we really are, rather than recognizing that we have a pure, stable, kind, and loving true nature that abides outside of the ego's charades.

When we identify with our ego, it stays intact and continues to run the show. Our ego would have us believe that we are a separate person in a disconnected body and mind that moves throughout our days, eating toast and driving around and answering emails, starring in the daily dramas of our lives. When we use inquiry in meditation, we can begin to see that the ego is created by our thoughts, and without our thoughts, there is no ego—only our true nature that is not separate from anything else in the universe.

Imposter Syndrome is what we call a particular collection of thoughts, when they appear in a certain way. When we start to lovingly question those thoughts, they dissolve in the warm water of inquiry, like spun sugar castles in a rain shower. They can't hold up.

When we're afraid to look directly at our own thoughts and feelings, we call that resistance, which is a word for the ego defending itself. As Byron Katie says, "Fear is the ego fighting for its life." All resistance, all fighting, all war is defense against feeling things we don't want to feel, against suffering. The wonderful news is that all suffering is created by our own thoughts, which means that we can find a way out of our suffering.

When we can awaken to this truth, we can welcome any thought or feeling with love and understanding. Through loving inquiry, we can wake up to the truth that only the ego can have hurt feelings or feel small or feel unworthy. Only the ego can hold on to this collection of thoughts and feelings that we call Imposter Syndrome. In fact, the ego is the original Imposter, masquerading as "me" when my true nature is not a separate "I" at all.

This is what "Love thy neighbor as thyself" truly means—there is no self separate from neighbor. I am my neighbor, and my neighbor is me. Until we awaken from the dream that we mistake for "me" and "my life," our ego fights hard to keep its job, mostly by keeping us afraid.

What do we require to go inward and question our thinking, to sit with our feelings instead of pushing them away or numbing them or distracting ourselves from them? Courage.

Facing Our Fears

Many years ago, when I was in my twenties and just out of grad school, one of my first jobs was as a case manager for adjudicated youth with alcohol or other drug addictions. I was part of a grant project that brought people from many disciplines and agencies together to figure out how to serve these youth more effectively in our community. Two of the team members were from the school district, and they invited me to go with them to present our work at a national conference. I was thrilled to be asked, and as we planned, I grew increasingly nervous as I realized that I'd be speaking in front of potentially hundreds of people, something I'd never done before.

Both of my responses were ego reactions. We tend to seek out and even chase after other people's positive regard and approval. We even say, "What an ego boost!" when we're picked to be on the team. Conversely, we try really hard to keep ourselves protected against anything we experience as negative feedback, criticism, or disapproval. What a perfect recipe for Imposter Syndrome.

Here I was, young and relatively inexperienced, not a public speaker or a professor with a PhD, having been a case manager for all of one year. Who was I to speak to a room full of people, most of whom were more credentialed and experienced than me? In my Imposter Syndrome thinking, I was *not* thinking about my own Master's degree, the years of experience I did have working with teens, and the good work I'd previously done. In other words, I thought only about what I lacked and not at all about what I had to offer. Those dreaded words from my childhood echoed in my head and heart: "Who do you think you are?"

When I expressed my fears and worries to my co-presenters, who were both older and wiser than me, they helped me by inviting me to consider "What's the worst that can happen?" I pondered for a bit and responded, "I'll freeze up, forget what to say, and they'll laugh at me." They said, "Okay, let's go with that." We continued to talk, and they helped me realize that if the worst thing I can imagine is people I don't know and will never see again laughing at me for a moment, then I am really lucky. They asked me if I'd experienced anything worse than that in my life and lived. As you know by now, I had lived through far worse things in my life and lived to tell the tale.

Poof! My fears relaxed their grip, and I was able to truly be present and relaxed enough to enjoy the whole process. I felt wonderful during our presentation and actually had fun! While I had some jitters right before we turned on our mics and stood up, it was just the kind of healthy adrenaline rush that gives us an edge to perform well, and not at all the mortal dread of Imposter Syndrome.

This early experience of questioning my fears and freeing myself of them never left me, even though it didn't cure me of Imposter Syndrome for the rest of my life. The lasting gift I received from that experience is the awareness that loving, compassionate inquiry into my own distorted thinking can free me from the ego's impulse to protect itself.

Are You Missing Your Own Life?

The ego's need to protect itself from anything less than approval and adoration is what's at play when we find ourselves playing small. I could easily have said, "No, that's okay," when my colleagues asked me to present with them. I don't recall the actual conversation, but I wouldn't be surprised if they actually had needed to convince me to say yes.

When we allow ego-driven fear to influence us, we miss out on life itself. This can happen in hundreds of ways. We drink too much, shop beyond our budgets, game for hours, binge on Netflix—we can find any number of ways to distract ourselves from how we feel when we don't like how we feel. We can avoid anything that even has the possibility to bring up feelings we don't want to have. We don't ask someone out because we fear they'll turn us down. We don't ask for the raise, we don't volunteer for the project, we don't accept the lunch invitation to keep our egos safe from any possibility of rejection or being seen as inadequate or unlikable or, or, or. We miss our own lives when we say, "I'm dreading presenting the report at the meeting this afternoon and can't wait until it's over." If we knew that we were going to die that evening in a car accident on the way home from work, would we have that thought, to wish away an hour of precious life, lost to fear? Or would we want to savor each and every delicious minute of being alive?

We continually forget that we will die someday, maybe sooner than we'd wish.

Ten years ago, I had a coaching client named Julie who breezed into my life like a breath of fresh air. She was full of life, had a sparkle in her eye, was game for anything, and said what she thought without reservation, not afraid to bring up her ugly and petty thoughts as she strove for well-being. I was always happy to see her and learned more about myself and life each time we met for coaching, almost always over delicious food at her favorite restaurant. She knew how to taste and savor life!

Over time, we became friends. One day in June, Julie sent an email to say she needed to reschedule our lunch date. She had a doctor's appointment to figure out why she couldn't shake a cold she'd had for over a month. By August she was gone, succumbing to the advanced lung cancer they found too late. When I think I'm having a bad day or I'm feeling like things aren't going my way or Imposter Syndrome is whispering to me to turn down an amazing opportunity, I remember Julie. I think, "Julie would give anything to have my 'bad day' right now. She'd give anything to have this opportunity." She continues to live within me to remind me that all we have is now, this moment, to live fully without fear.

Loving Our Fears, Opening to Joy

The world-renowned Buddhist master teacher Thich Nhat Hahn advises us to respond to our thoughts and feelings as a mother would respond to her beloved baby, with nurturing tenderness, cradling them gently in our arms. Indeed, we truly are the mothers who create and give birth to all of our thoughts, so we can have a mother's love toward them.

It is this loving welcome that dissolves the ego's resistance. Byron Katie has similar advice, saying that our thoughts are like needy children begging for our attention—See me! See me!—deserving our love even as we let them go.

The ego's misguided efforts to protect us from feeling anything unpleasant can keep us from feeling elation and happiness as well. When we numb some feelings, we numb them all.

When we become free from ego and Imposter Syndrome, we can experience the full range of our feelings without fear, and we open ourselves to joy.

Touchstone Practice: Be Brave and Courageous

Fortunately, there are many resources available to us to do this work of mindful inquiry into the thoughts that keep us living small, caught in a dream rather than being fully alive and awake in the present moment. We can engage in study on our own, utilizing the internet and libraries to explore the many books, podcasts, and videos available to us. We can journal or meditate on our own to begin to question our thoughts and feelings and turn them around. A book I have found particularly helpful is Mare Chapman's *Unshakeable Confidence, the Freedom to Be Our Authentic Selves: Mindfulness for Women*.

Often, it's helpful to have someone else help us with this work because we are so close to and identified with our thinking that it's hard to see clearly or differently. We can find a skilled therapist, coach, or spiritual advisor to help us sort out our thinking and heal our wounds. Many offer a sliding scale, and many communities have resources for helping those of us with low incomes afford mental health services. We can find local meditation groups through the internet, or even join an online meditation community. Many meditation groups don't charge fees but invite people to give what they can, as they are able.

I highly recommend *Love and Rage: The Path of Liberation Through Anger* by Lama Rod Owens as a guide for using our anger to get in touch with our underlying hurt, pain, and grief, and ultimately, finding our way to love and liberation. Through stories and clear, approachable language, he explains what meditation is and offers practices that help us to bravely face what we'd rather avoid.

Whatever way you choose, you may find that you need courage to start down the path. Imposter Syndrome may kick in, telling you that getting help is for the weak or that this is all just a bunch of new age nonsense, or other lies. Your ego will kick into high gear defense mode and say just about anything to keep you living in the ego's dreamworld rather than living an awake life of freedom. Have the courage to question, and you'll have all the courage you need to be free.

CHAPTER EIGHT

Walk in Integrity

That just doesn't sound like her.
They seem off to me—they wouldn't normally do that.
I wasn't myself when I said that.

We can sense when we or others step out of integrity.

Integrity is all about being whole and sound in character, adhering to a code of principles, ethics, and values that we believe in with all our hearts. We have a personal North Star to follow.

Polaris, more commonly known as the North Star, has been guiding people for centuries. What's unique about Polaris is that, unlike other stars, it never changes position and always points north. As one of the highest stars in the sky, it is a steady, reliable wayfinder in the heavens. Early seafarers used Polaris to estimate their position in vast oceans with nothing but water visible from horizon to horizon. Overland travelers used it to navigate familiar routes and to track their way in unknown territory. In the U.S., enslaved Blacks followed Polaris north to freedom, saving their very lives. The words in the spiritual "Follow the Drinking Gourd" are a coded guide to the route along major waterways, through forests and hills, always heading northward.

> *The river ends between two hills*
> *Follow the Drinking Gourd.*
> *There's another river on the other side*
> *Follow the Drinking Gourd.*

Today, when we talk about having a personal North Star, we mean that we have a guide for our lives that doesn't waver, one that is clear and bright and unchanged by external influences. We have an internal guide to freedom.

What is Integrity Worth?

In the early years of my consulting practice, I frequently worked within the public school system, particularly with groups of educators who wanted to start small schools that were innovative or served students whose needs weren't met by traditional schooling. The Wisconsin Department of Public Instruction offered start-up grants to support educational innovation, and I'd become an expert at working collaboratively with teams to successfully apply for and be awarded grant funding. It was labor-intensive work, so each year, I selected a few teams who were creating a school that I could believe in and wanted to support.

One summer, I went to an informational meeting at a suburban school district that served primarily white students in an affluent community. The Superintendent, an older white man who'd been in the District for many years, told me that he was prepared to pay me $40,000 to apply for grant funding using a school model that a consulting colleague of mine had developed for them. I felt grateful that he understood the value of a consultant's time and expertise and was interested in hearing more about the deliverables.

Then, to my complete shock, he came right out and told me that once they got the money, they didn't actually plan to start the school at all. The money would be spent to outfit a single state-of-the-art classroom for twenty students as part of a prestigious STEM (science, technology, engineering, math) program that required a specific and costly classroom lab setup. As I listened with growing incredulity, he explained how he'd engineer the bait and switch.

One of the grant requirements mandated the formation of an independent Governance Board to provide oversight and be legally accountable for following all rules, laws, and regulations. He planned to fill this Board with his cronies. He literally nudged me and winked as he said, "If you pick the right people, they'll vote yes on anything you tell them to."

I know my colleague would be horrified that her work would be used in this unethical scheme, and this man sorely underestimated me. It surprises me to this day that some people think we consultants are desperate for work and money and will do anything they ask. He was under the illusion that the $40,000 price tag was one I couldn't refuse.

I kept my cool in the meeting and asked if he minded if I consulted the grant program leaders to inquire about some of his questions on his behalf. "Sure, go ahead! We go way back." He was counting on their complicity, too. I told him I'd be in touch and left the building.

As soon as I got back to my home office, I wrote two emails. One was to him to say that I was not interested in working with him, and one was to the leaders of the grant program who I also knew quite well to alert them to what the Superintendent was planning, Since he hadn't actually done anything wrong at that point, there were no consequences for his egregious behavior, but they told him he should withdraw his application. They also told me that at the beginning of their conversation with him, he expressed frustration and disbelief that I'd turned him down. "Who turns down forty grand?"

People with integrity, that's who.

Integrity is the Backbone of Character

Allowing ourselves to think, act, or speak in ways that aren't in line with our values and moral code is one of the quickest ways to activate Imposter Syndrome because we are literally not being ourselves.

Picture your spine, with all its vertebrae lined up as they should be. Now imagine one of the vertebrae slipping out of place (some of you have had this actual experience). When our spine isn't aligned, we can experience pain and discomfort or even paralysis. We are in a state of dis-ease. Now imagine a skilled physical therapist or chiropractor helping us adjust our spine back into alignment, and the feelings of relief, comfort, and ease that follows.

When we feel uneasy, we can check to see if we've stepped off the path, no longer following the North Star of our values.

I've had that queasy feeling myself a number of times in my life. I am embarrassed to admit these things, but I'm committed to being vulnerable in this book, so here goes:

- I found a beautiful women's watch on the floor behind a floor model couch at a furniture store, and I kept it.
- I betrayed a confidence and told a secret that wasn't mine to tell in order to get someone to like me.
- I lied and made up a story about bad weather to get an airline ticket refunded, when really, I'd just changed my plans.
- I spent an hour venting about someone to a coworker, then denied that anything was wrong when that person asked me if I was mad at them.

Being a consultant has helped teach me the value of integrity. Keeping my conduct beyond reproach is essential for my success. Tarnishing it would affect not just me, but my clients. If I'm indicted for questionable or illegal business conduct, everyone on my client list is at risk of being judged poorly because of their affiliation with me. I've also established a reputation for admitting what I don't know and never trying to bluff my way into a consulting contract. If I do not have the skills or expertise a prospective client needs, I'm the first to say so, and I connect them with a consultant who does.

There are many ways, whether we judge them as big or small or defensible or not, that we can slip out of alignment. Once we do, if we have a well-developed conscience, we feel dis-ease set in. We have become less trustworthy not only to others but to ourselves.

The Discomfort of Dissonance

Retired Hall of Fame basketball coach John Wooden said, "The true test of a man's character is what he does when no one is watching." Someone is always watching, though, and it's not Santa. It's you.

Cognitive dissonance is a psychological term that means "the state of having inconsistent thoughts, beliefs, or attitudes, especially as relating to behavioral decisions and attitude change." If I see myself as a moral and ethical person, and I tell myself that "I never lie" or "I am always 100% upfront," I create cognitive dissonance for myself when I lie. And let's face it—it is terribly difficult to get through the day without lying in some way.

Researchers find varying results on how often we lie (anywhere between two and twenty times a day), but they all agree that people lie on a daily basis. If we then lie to ourselves about our lying, we create dissonance between our actions and our beliefs. Cognitive dissonance is fertile ground for Imposter Syndrome.

As we've discussed earlier, we humans are generally trying to increase our chances of feeling good and avoid feeling bad. We slip and slide on our morals and ethics when we're trying to get something we want, get someone to do what we want, or get away with something we've convinced ourselves we deserve, to name a few motivations. The more we do this, the less we trust ourselves, so even in situations where we're acting ethically and morally, the feeling of being shady eats away at us.

The Road to Freedom

I have learned that as long as I hold fast to my beliefs and values, and follow my own moral compass, then the only expectations I need to live up to are my own.
—Michelle Obama

If we want to live a principled and truthful life in accordance with our values (i.e. if we want to Walk in Integrity), we have to get really clear about what our values actually are. It is really helpful to identify our top five to ten values and know why they matter to us.

Companies and organizations do this all the time, but I rarely come across leaders, teams, or individuals who have done this for themselves. When I suggest it, people usually love the idea and say, "Of course! Why didn't I ever think to do that?" But a funny thing happens—about half the people never get around to doing the work, and a year later, more than half of the ones who did cannot remember what they came up with.

I'd like to suggest that you not only take the time to define your personal values, but that you put your written list of values in a prominent place where you can see it each and every day. One person I know carries his list around in his wallet. Others put it in their blog or on their LinkedIn profile page. Others put it up on their cubicle wall or tape it to their computer monitor. Do what works for you.

Keeping our values visible is exactly what we mean when we talk about "following your North Star." It's really hard to follow Polaris if you never look up to orient yourself by its light.

Will you have the courage to follow your North Star, even when the going gets tough? When no one but you will know? When it could cost you a job? When it would be far more convenient not to? Will you have the courage to look honestly at yourself and admit when you've lost your way?

The beautiful thing about learning to Walk in Integrity is that no matter how far off course we may wander, we can always find our way back. Search within your soul for Polaris, your inner North Star, and find your way to freedom.

Touchstone Practice: Walk in Integrity

Exercise: Defining Your Values

Step One: Remember a time – a day, an hour, a week – when you felt you were at your best. Let yourself sink into that memory. Really put yourself back in that moment, as if you were in that time. What feelings do you have? What actions are you taking? What are you thinking and feeling about yourself? How are you relating with other people?

Take out a notebook to write about it, talk out loud to yourself, or make sketches – anything to help you with remembering. If you want to spark your thinking, go to the internet and search "list of personal values" to see how to put values into words that resonate with you.

Step Two: Here is a list of additional questions that can help make your values visible.

1. Where and how do you spend your time and resources?
2. What kind of work or volunteering do you do, either paid or unpaid?
3. What kinds of people do you like to spend time with?
4. When do you experience flow (being absorbed in an activity, losing track of time)?
5. Who do you admire?
6. When do you feel most alive?
7. What gives you a feeling of peace?
8. What would your best friend tell you about yourself?
9. When do you feel most useful to others?
10. What are you most proud of in your life?

Step Three: Keep adding to your list until you have a set of 5-10 values that feels complete. Post it where you will see it each day, and consider sharing it with others, too.

CHAPTER NINE

Honor Honesty

*Truth and courage aren't always comfortable,
but they're never weakness.*
—Brené Brown

Honesty. When we think about being honest, we usually think about not telling lies to other people. That's definitely important. But as we've seen with the other Touchstones, when it comes to Imposter Syndrome, we have to start with ourselves first. If we can't be honest with ourselves, we can't be authentic and honest with others.

Why would we lie to ourselves? Actually, the reasons aren't all that different than the reasons we have for lying to others—to avoid an unpleasant consequence. A classic example is a toddler with cookie crumbs all over their face, vehemently insisting, "I didn't eat a cookie!" The kiddo is trying to avoid getting in trouble or feeling bad for doing something that they knew they weren't supposed to do by avoiding the truth. In their imagination, telling the truth is not going to end with a pleasant outcome.

As adults, the scenarios may be more sophisticated, but our motivations aren't so different. We seek out what we like or want and try to avoid what we don't. Let's consider a story to see how this works.

Ronda is in the heady early days of dating Justine, the Communications Director at a progressive political action organization that she joined several months ago. Ronda is completely infatuated with her. When Justine asks her if she would be her date and accompany her to the formal Board dinner where she'll be unveiling their latest campaign communications plan, she's thrilled to be invited to a special event where she can see her sweetheart in action. After the presentation, Justine joins Ronda at the bar where she is downing a martini. Justine says, "I think that went really well! What do you think?" The truth is that Ronda found it painful to watch Justine's lackluster performance and could see that the Board was, frankly, bored as well. She has been dreading this moment, hence the martini.

What do you think she should do?

Dilemmas like this one present themselves to us all the time in the course of our daily lives, and the reason they're dilemmas is because there isn't a clear answer that is empirically right or wrong. We believe we're choosing between equally unpleasant outcomes. When asked what we think someone in a dilemma should do, we usually want to say, "Well, it depends on _____." What we put in the blank is influenced by our experiences, identities, values, personality, culture, beliefs, religion, and other influences. The consequences are weightier and more complex than risking a time out for stealing a cookie.

In our example, Ronda may believe that she has to choose between hurting Justine's feelings and going against her values by lying. Ronda could avoid the dilemma by convincing herself that she actually did love the presentation. She can tell herself, "I'm not a communications expert so there must be something I'm not understanding yet," or "I never met the Board before so I may not be reading them correctly," or "Justine is smart and talented, and she has been so successful, so my reaction after one experience isn't really valid." Ronda hugs Justine and says, "It was amazing!"

So what does Ronda's decision have to do with Imposter Syndrome? Everything! When we develop the habit of pushing away our feelings, second-guessing our opinions, and questioning our own sense of reality to avoid uncomfortable situations or risk losing other people's approval, we learn to not trust ourselves. We *are* untrustworthy, and we know it.

Small Lies, Smaller Lives

The ways we lie to ourselves would make a list longer than this book, or maybe 10,000 books. Think about your favorite TV shows, movies, books—almost always, a character gets themselves in trouble by lying to themselves. As you read or watch, you might even yell at them. "Come on! Stop kidding yourself!" or "Come on! Just tell them what you really feel!" We can recognize this habit in others because we can recognize it in ourselves.

There's nothing like being an imposter to trigger a good case of Imposter Syndrome.

It's beyond the scope of this chapter to delve into the myriad ways and reasons we lie to ourselves. There are whole fields devoted to understanding and even capitalizing on this oh-so-human tendency—philosophy, psychology, ethics, advertising, politics. I'd like to hone in on the kind of lying that we saw Ronda do in our example, which is convincing ourselves to disregard what we know to be true to escape taking responsibility for our thoughts, feelings, words, and actions.

We know from research that our tendency is to make valid excuses for our own mistakes while blaming others' failures on their character. This is known as Fundamental Attribution Error. For example, when I miss a deadline and turn in a report late, I might excuse myself to my boss by saying, "I didn't have my report done on time because I was so busy helping the art department get the graphics right." But when my coworker Jacob misses a deadline, I am likely to think and even say, "If Jacob wasn't such a slacker, he would have had his report done last week."

It can be really hard to see this tendency in ourselves. In fact, you might be thinking right now, "I don't do that." I invite you to look again, to see if there isn't some area of your life where you aren't being completely honest with yourself.

We do ourselves harm when we are not honest with ourselves, especially when we develop narratives about who we are and who we are not. We often accept these stories about ourselves as True with a capital T as if they are solid, immutable facts. Because we believe them so fully, we may not even question them. This puts us at risk for missing out on opportunities and living smaller lives.

Here are examples of stories masquerading as fact that I've heard from myself, clients, friends, and loved ones:

I could never give a talk at our industry conference—I can't speak in front of crowds.

If my ex hadn't been such a jerk, I wouldn't have such a hard time dating now.

I'm always the person on the outside of the group. I'm different from everyone.

If they would only do their part, then maybe I wouldn't be so grumpy at work every day.

I would never go to dinner at a fancy restaurant by myself—that's like advertising, "Hey! Pathetic person here!"

If you were abused like I was, you wouldn't trust anyone, either.

I'll never get that promotion because my co-manager is so much more likable than I am. I just can't compete with that.

She says I'm the problem in the relationship, but I'm fine—she's just insecure.

I can't believe my 360 report says that I don't listen. I do nothing but listen to people all day!

If you get really quiet and take time to do some mindful inquiry, I think you'd be surprised at what may come up on your list of stories you tell about yourself that you'd swear are Absolutely True for Very Good Reasons.

Speaking the Unspeakable

As I admitted before, one of the reasons I was hesitant to share stories about my early life experiences is that I don't want to be perceived to be making excuses for my many poor choices and the hurtful things I've done in my life. I've had people actually say to me, "You can't blame your life on your parents."

Admittedly, I've usually heard that from people who didn't have my best interests at heart or had something going on that had nothing to do with me. But I think, in one way, my defensive reaction was sparked by my agreement with those folks (although I didn't appreciate being on the receiving end of their unsolicited advice). What I wanted to snap back was, "I know! I'm trying! You don't know what I've lived through!"

What I believe now is that my life was profoundly affected by my parents *and* that I am responsible for my life. To be clear, this is not to say that we don't have healing work to do when we've experienced trauma or hardship or tragedy. It is to say that part of becoming an adult is realizing that the work of healing is ours to do.

I used to think that if my parents sincerely admitted their wrongs and asked for my forgiveness, I would be free and happy. It drives me nuts when TV shows and movies depict scenes in which "child confronts parent about how they hurt them, parent cries, begs forgiveness," because that rarely happens in real life. It certainly didn't happen in mine.

When I was in graduate school, I went to therapy to deal with the truth that I'd kept to myself for so long. I'd never told anyone about what happened to me or how afraid I was to be in my home. My friends saw signs now and then, when I'd walk into school with my mouth bleeding or with an angry red scratch down my neck, but I was too ashamed to talk about what was really happening in my home. Shame is a powerful silencer.

I had a teenage sister at home who I worried about constantly. I didn't want the sexual abuse that happened to me to happen to her, although I knew she was capable of exploding in anger and might be more capable of defending herself, compared to me, who went quiet, passive, and invisible. I thought I had to protect her, and I thought if I told the truth, I could keep her safe. I wrote a letter that told the truth about the sexual abuse (and other abuses), and with equal parts determination and terror, sent it to my parents, brother, sister, and grandmother.

In my youthful naivete, I imagined that everyone would rally around and comfort me, condemn my father, and demand that he get treatment. What actually happened is that everyone was incredibly pissed off—at me. My brother said that maybe he remembered some things that would back up what I said, but wouldn't speak out because he didn't want to take sides. My sister was angry because she had to live with them after what I stirred up. My grandmother, who loved me dearly, begged me to just forget it all because "there are things I'll take to my grave and won't ever tell," so the family could stay together. My parents joined the False Memory Syndrome Society (yes, that's a real thing), sent letters to my friends and parents-in-law telling them I was sick and needed help. My mother started sending me letters with things like "Happy Memories for Jenni", listing all the good things they'd ever done for me. I opened a box to find it full of my childhood toys, bringing back a flood of emotion that made me vomit.

The next holiday, they all gathered together, and I was on the outside, alone. No one asked me how I was, what I needed, or offered support. To explain this unimaginable outcome to myself, I came up with a lot of stories about myself and my life that took a long time and a lot of therapy to unravel and unlearn. Things I thought were true were:

I'm unlovable and shouldn't expect to be loved.

No one will protect me or defend me.

If my own family can treat me so badly, then I deserve no better from others.

My truth will make people abandon me.

My words cause harm.

As understandable as my reactions may be, the reality is that I was the one to think them, so I was the only one who could unthink them.

I've come to believe what Viktor Frankl famously said: "Everything can be taken from a [person] but one thing: the last of the human freedoms—to choose one's attitude in any given set of circumstances, to choose one's own way."

All along in those darkest of times, my good and pure true nature was there, obscured behind storm clouds like a bright shining moon. I caught glimpses of my shining true nature often enough to keep holding on, to keep trying, to not give in to suicide and find a better life for myself. There was always a voice in me I could hear saying, "There is another way to live."

Unlearning Lies, Reclaiming Our Power

As a reminder, Imposter Syndrome is believing that we do not deserve or that we have not rightfully earned the success we've had despite all the evidence to the contrary. It is believing we shouldn't be at the table and worrying that at any moment, everyone else will realize it.

For years, I saddled myself with a persistent belief that had an enormous impact on my professional life and definitely contributed to Imposter Syndrome: *If my own family can treat me so badly, then I deserve no better from others.*

This belief, like most disempowering beliefs, was born out of a *story* which I mistakenly confused with *reality*. As you can imagine, believing this thought was detrimental to my professional (and personal) life because I had an extremely hard time standing up for myself. I accepted all kinds of poor treatment from others, which took a toll on my emotional, physical, and spiritual well-being. I was being an imposter by pretending that everything was okay and nothing was wrong when others treated me badly. I had lost my voice, in part because of my other belief, *My words cause harm.*

In my late twenties, I was working at a high school as a counselor. I was struggling on many fronts in my life. My marriage was ending because of constant infidelities, and I was burned out from being a caretaker for a partner who struggled with crippling depression and suicidal impulses. I was trying to complete my master's thesis after long days of working with young people who were dealing with the hardest, saddest, most unfair circumstances you can imagine. When you work with people with addictions, inevitably some of them will die, and the funerals shook me. My friend circle had collapsed because my husband hit on my friends, and no one wanted to spend time with us.

It was during this time that a male colleague began to make sexual advances. It started out looking like friendship—he would listen to my struggles and show concern, as any friend would. In time, he began flirting. That felt good at the time because I was feeling unlovable, unattractive, and rejected. The flirting led to shoulder rubs, and then one day, he slid his hands down my chest. I froze, and I let him. *If my own family can treat me so badly, then I deserve no better from others*,

It never occurred to me that he was out of line. I was an adult, and I'd allowed the situation to get this far. I took all the blame. It definitely didn't occur to me to talk to my principal, a woman who in retrospect would have fiercely defended me and taken disciplinary action. In the early 90's, I don't know if the words "sexual harassment" were as commonly spoken in the workplace, but even if they were, my unquestioned beliefs would likely have still kept me silent:

I'm unlovable and shouldn't expect to be loved.

No one will protect me or defend me.

If my own family can treat me so badly, then I deserve no better from others.

My truth will make people abandon me.

My words cause harm.

When we don't tell the truth to ourselves and to others, we will be less likely to show up as powerful, confident, and effective professionals. When we are afraid and ashamed, as I was, we are less likely to confidently ask for a raise, put our hat in the ring to be part of a new initiative, or see ourselves as a capable leader. We are more likely to live in the dark shadow of Imposter Syndrome, fearful that other people will discover our secret—that despite all of our good work, we are not worthy.

While all of this was going on, I still managed to excel in my role. My supervisor led us in a research project to help demonstrate that our work was effective, and my data showed that students in my program were statistically significantly improving after engagement—they had fewer truancies and behavioral referrals, their grades went up, and they were more likely to graduate. I created over a dozen new programs and was invited to sit on community councils working on the toughest problems in my community. I passed my thesis defense and could claim the title M.A.

But despite all of my hard work and success, I felt as ashamed and invisible and undeserving as ever. And also as ever, I could still hear that quiet, wise voice inside, like catching a strain of music wafting by on a breeze: "There's another way to live..." Those moments of grace swept the storm clouds away from the face of the moon just enough for me to catch glimpses of myself the way my supervisors and colleagues saw me.

Those glimpses were enough to keep me searching and seeking for that better way. With the help of therapists, loving friends, books, and retreats, I began to question what I thought was true. I started to heal.

In Search of Higher Ground

"Discomfort is always a necessary part of enlightenment."
—*Pearl Cleage*

Right now, your ego may be really nervous, and you may notice that you're feeling uncomfortable. Maybe you even want to stop reading or skip this chapter. Ego depends on us believing our thoughts, and mistakenly believing that our thoughts are true. We can begin to feel anything from uneasiness to stark terror when we start to question our belief systems, to open up to not knowing. Creating cracks in the foundation of our familiar belief system can feel scary, unsettling, and dangerous. As you recall from the start of this chapter, wanting to avoid unpleasantness is one of our primary motivations for lying to ourselves and others, so we may want to pull the blanket back over our heads at this point and remain in the dark.

I'd like to propose a radical idea—that it's okay to be uncomfortable. I had a wonderful coach for several years who liked to say, "It's much better to deal with things as they are than how we wish they were." I didn't always want to agree with him on that because sometimes reality seemed unbearably uncomfortable, but I came to learn that the pain and discomfort of building my life on empty wishes and avoiding reality was ultimately far worse.

You may already understand that what we see in the mirror of self-honesty may not always be easy to look at. We might be embarrassed or ashamed when we see parts of us that aren't what we consider to be our best selves. We can call upon the other Touchstones and remember that just like everyone else, we are learning. We are healing. We are imperfect.

Remember, we don't have to be perfect to be lovable and worthy. Think about someone you truly admire—do you admire them because they're perfect? Or do you admire them more when you find out that actually, they also struggle with some of the same things you do? If we are to be emotionally mature, we do need to get really honest and take responsibility for those parts of ourselves, too.

I used to be a chameleon. In an effort to be liked and fit in as a young adult, I would take on the interests, opinions, tastes, and styles of people I wanted to like and accept me. I spent hours on activities that I thought were boring and pretended to be fascinated. I wore clothes that I didn't really like to look more like the people I wanted as friends. If someone said, "What should we do tonight?", I waited for others to answer and went along with what they came up with. Instead of endearing me to people, I noticed that people were often irritated and annoyed by me. Once, on a college course trip, three of my friends actually ditched me when I was busy looking in a shop window so they could have lunch without me. I was mortified. I was caught in a cycle of shame and desperation: the worse I felt about myself, the more I tried to fit in; the more I annoyed people, the worse I felt about myself; and round and round I'd go.

In Chapter Three, I told the story about how I began to heal and recover from this cycle by getting to know my own mind, tastes, preferences, and opinions—and believing that I deserved to have and express them. The more "me" I became, the more I blossomed and created authentic friendships. The effect was deeper connection with others, which was what I had desired all along.

We can only have authentic connections with others when we can be trusted and trustworthy enough to tell the truth, and truth-telling must begin with ourselves. After all the pain, hard work, and discomfort of facing the truth about ourselves and our lives, we are rewarded when we pull ourselves out of the muck and mire to stand, at last, on higher ground.

Seeing Ourselves In the Mirror of Community

When we want to see how we look, we go and find a mirror. When we want to see ourselves more clearly, we can certainly see a lot of ourselves without a mirror, but there are some things that will remain out of our own sight that others can plainly see. Drawing on our other Touchstones, we can get courageous, be brave, and ask for help to accelerate and support our efforts to be more honest with ourselves.

We can embrace interdependence and accept that we are here to heal each other by healing ourselves, and that asking for help is the epitome of courage and generosity. As researcher, author, and speaker Brené Brown writes, "When you cannot accept and ask for help without self-judgment, then when you offer other people help, you are always doing so with judgment." Wow. Let that sink in for a minute.

One of the ways we can ask for help is to ask for feedback. Did you just shudder? I think what comes to mind for most of us when we hear the word "feedback" is receiving criticism—constructive or otherwise. We have a biological reflex against opening ourselves up to that. Our brains evolved to scan the environment continually and quickly for threats so we can defend ourselves against them, so our biology primes us to develop defensive mental habits that can be challenging to unlearn.

But first, a word of caution: **remember to Develop Discernment** (Chapter Two).

I once dated a man (as promised, the "a little humility is refreshing" guy from Chapter Two is back) who berated me when I correctly pointed in the direction of our hotel in New York City, despite never having been in NYC before. He demanded that I explain how I knew it was that way, and I couldn't in logical terms that made sense to his engineer brain. "I just know. Am I wrong?" I wasn't, and it drove him crazy that I didn't need to rely on him to get back. For all three days of what was supposed to be a fun, romantic Christmas in the City getaway, he intermittently sulked and kept trying to pick fights that honestly baffled me (although he did run out to get me ginger ale and PeptoBismol after some bad sushi, which was nice of him).

The next incident began in a bar when we met a colorful character who wanted to chat. He and I launched into a rollicking, wide-ranging conversation about everything from chefs to quantum physics to the best place to get gelato in Florence. We had a glorious time, and it's one of my favorite NYC memories to this day. Not for my boyfriend, however. When we left, I said, "That was so fun!" and he turned to me and said, "You're a liar. You can't possibly know all the things you said you did in that conversation."

I felt like he slapped me, which I guess he did, verbally. I got quiet for a while then said, "So one of two things is true. One, I was making things up, and if I was, so what? We were having fun and no harm was done. Or two, I do know all of those things, in which case, what does this conversation say about you?" He admitted that if I wasn't a liar, he'd be an ass. Ah, something we could agree on.

This all culminated in him not speaking to me on Christmas Day. He sat sipping coffee and reading the New York Times, chair turned away and pointedly not speaking to me. I was teary and miserable and wished I knew someone in NYC so I could escape and salvage the holiday.

I'm sharing this story to illustrate that some mirrors are like fun house mirrors, distorted and designed to make you smaller than you are, or uglier than you are. Be sure you choose mirrors that are well-balanced, clear, and sound. Be a good mirror for yourself and give your good qualities as much light as your flaws.

Honesty in Action

Choosing to be honest is the first step in the process of love.
There is no practitioner of love who deceives.
—bell hooks

I want to end this chapter by encouraging you to read *and then actually do* the practice in the next section. In many ways, it's a capstone exercise that brings together many, if not all, of the other Touchstones. Completing it may require courage because you'll be vulnerable. You'll need to embrace interdependence, practice discernment, and accept generosity. Your results may help you heal, and they may help you to create your list of values—your North Star to guide your sense of integrity.

I hope you take the opportunity to make an honest ask for honest feedback. Like any kind of skill, from piano to polo to pumpkin carving, we get better the more often we practice.

Touchstone Practice: Honor Honesty

Here is your mission, should you choose to accept it. Think of five to ten people who know you well and have your best interest at heart. Ask some of your nearest and dearest as well as someone who may not even be a close friend, but who you trust to have good intentions toward you. Here's a sample email to send:

> Hi _____,
>
> I've been reading a book about Imposter Syndrome, and in it, there's a chapter about learning to see ourselves more clearly. I decided to do one of the recommended exercises, and that's where I need your help.
>
> The assignment is to contact several trusted friends and colleagues who know me well and who I trust to give me honest feedback.

Here is the assignment question: What do you see as my top five talents, gifts, or strengths?

As someone I both trust and respect, I would be grateful for your feedback, if you are willing and able.

Thank you so much for your time and support.

(Your Name)

Some of you are already heading for your device to compose the email and hit send. Others of you are breaking into a cold sweat at the mere thought of doing this. If that's you, you're not alone, and I invite you to reach for the Touchstone in Chapter Seven: Be Brave and Courageous.

I first did this exercise myself thirteen years ago, and I still have the responses I received. I went searching for them as I wrote this chapter and was delighted to find them in an old file. The words these generous souls wrote touch me now as much as they did then, only now, I have so much more capacity to believe them. Each word rings just as true, but now, the resonance reaches my soul.

After you complete the first challenge of sending the emails out, the next challenge is to read the feedback you receive and believe it. Really take in what you hear and find in yourself the qualities people are reflecting back to you. Look into the mirror they're holding up with open, self-loving eyes. Do your friends and acquaintances justice by choosing to Honor Honesty—both theirs, and yours.

CHAPTER TEN

Create Space

"Until you value yourself, you will not value your time."
—M. Scott Peck

You've held nine Touchstones in your heart and mind at this point.

The tenth Touchstone is like compost for your garden. Everything will grow fine without it, but with it, everything will flourish and bloom that much better. The compost for our work on overcoming Imposter Syndrome is something you can't hold in your hands but is worth more than gold: space.

I wrote a blog post a couple of years ago called, 'Busy is the New Fine." When someone asks us how we are by way of greeting, we used to say, "Fine, thank you." Now we say, "Busy!" We wear it like a badge of honor, practically bragging about how full our calendars are, how many errands we squeezed in, how little sleep we got, and how many after-school activity runs we have to make before we can put the finishing touches on the team's presentation at 11 pm. I'm exhausted just writing that sentence.

Stop the madness.
Take a breath.
Slow down.

I don't believe that we have an information problem. We know that we're supposed to have "me time," take breaks, go to yoga, light a candle and soak in a tub, meditate for twenty minutes a day. We've seen the words "self-care" more times than we can count in our feeds and online article headlines. We even have catchy expressions:

You can't pour water from an empty cup.

Put your own oxygen mask on first.

An empty tank will get you nowhere.

No one has ever said, "Take care of myself? That's crazy talk." It is not news to anyone that regular exercise, a good diet, proper sleep, and meditation have profound effects on our mental, emotional, and physical wellbeing. We know that these practices can boost the immune system, maintain low blood pressure, alleviate anxiety or depression, and even improve our interpersonal relationships. So if we have all the information we need about what is good for us, what keeps us running and working and scheduling every waking moment or filling our downtime with screen time, binge watching the latest series, or scrolling through our feeds for hours?

Driving Ourselves to Distraction

I think there are two things at play.

One, we are doing our best to distract ourselves from experiencing discomfort, which we've seen is a motivator for all kinds of less than healthy behavior. We keep busy and binge on media, food, drink, or activity to avoid facing our darker thoughts and feelings that come to our awareness when we pause and are still.

Two, we have been taught not to say no to anyone, except to ourselves.

When I say yes to driving early morning carpool, I'm saying no to the delicious time in bed when I think my best thoughts and beginning my day with a surge of inspiration that follows me to my home office. When I say yes to meeting up for drinks on a Wednesday, I'm saying no to my meditation practice with my sangha (a community that meditates together). When I say yes to a client because they say they can only meet at 10 am on Thursday, I say no to my beloved yoga class that meets at that same time.

Saying no to others and yes to ourselves can be hard for anyone, but I think it's especially hard for those of us who are woman-identifying and were raised as girls. We were raised to put our needs last and accommodate others in service to being nice and pleasing and pleasant. If you have the additional layer of growing up with abuse, addiction, mental illness, or other trauma, you may have learned that it wasn't safe to say no. You may have some healing and learning to do, and you may need support as we practice this self-and life-affirming word of *No*.

Imposter Syndrome Creeps In When We're Worn Out

As a stepmom, I've faced particular kinds of stressors that only other stepmoms can truly understand. I've devoured whole books and read every article on stepmom stress that's been written this century. If I had a dollar for every time I read, "Get a mani-pedi", I could pay for a year's worth of mani-pedis. That advice just made me want to scream. Were they serving dirty martinis and providing a therapist for that hour? [Sidenote: I finally went and got a mani-pedi to see if I was wrong. Although I enjoyed my pretty blue toenails, it didn't live up to the hype for me. If it works for you, definitely go!]

The kind of taking space that I want to write about goes beyond a bubble bath and a cup of hot chocolate, although those are delightful comforts that we shouldn't deny ourselves. I'm talking about having the courage to fiercely protect our non-working hours. To hold sacred the time we put on the calendar to move and strengthen our bodies. To be rigorously honest with our yes and our no, so we don't take on obligations or social commitments that we later resent or regret.

When we are exhausted, irritable, resentful, and burned out, we leave ourselves far more susceptible to Imposter Syndrome.

To go back to our garden metaphor, if we don't feed and water a garden well, it is stressed and susceptible to parasites, fungus, and all manner of ills that weaken the plants and their ability to blossom or produce fruit. When we're running ourselves ragged and are overcommitted, we leave ourselves vulnerable to self-doubt, insecurity, self-consciousness, anxiety, low self-esteem, and physical illness.

When we have those feelings running, we are most susceptible to comparison which is like Miracle-Gro for Imposter Syndrome. We look around and believe that other people are balancing their lives easily, going to lunchtime yoga and landing the account with ease. We believe that others have it all together and are there for everyone in their lives, seamlessly running a major campaign while not missing their niece's ballet recital or their third cousin's daughter's bat mitzvah. When we compare ourselves to others and find ourselves coming up short, we are playing on Imposter Syndrome's home field.

Saying Yes to Yourself

Among my friends and colleagues, I'm known for setting healthy boundaries on my capacity and not overworking myself. For me, keeping my working hours in check is a spiritual practice, rooted in my values and guiding principles (see Chapter Eight: Walk in Integrity).

When I became a self-employed coach and consultant, I discovered that most people hold the misconception that anyone who is self-employed must be working like a dog, putting in 50, 60, or even 70 hours a week in order to be successful. To this day, people say things to me like, "I love having my regular paycheck and 40-hour week, thank you very much. That's not for me." I admit that I enjoy seeing their jaws drop when I tell them that I work between 25-30 hours most weeks and take almost two months off each year, and that I leave my office in the middle of the day to go paddling or hiking if sunshine and blue skies beckon. Sure, I have major projects or deadlines now and then when I pour it on, but not for too long a stretch at any one time.

This wasn't always the case, particularly when I was employed and still striving to get approval from others. I wanted to please my boss, be known as someone who got the job done, and went above and beyond at any opportunity. As you likely know, there is ample reward for being this way in our culture. We are encouraged to be "the first one in, the last one out" and are told "you can sleep when you're dead," even though we know that death will come earlier if we don't sleep.

One of the first things I did when I started my business was to write down my guiding principles, one of which is "Be a good boss to myself." This means not working when I'm sick, taking lots of vacations, not working on weekends or in the evening, taking a personal day when I'm worn out, and putting what I call my "anchor events" in my calendar *first* and scheduling work around them. My yoga class goes in my calendar before anything else. When someone asks me to come to a meeting at that same time, my answer is a simple, "Sorry, I'm not available."

I say yes to myself, which sometimes means saying no to others. And you know what that makes me? In the language of the Touchstones, it makes me Honest and Brave. It means I Walk in Integrity. It means I continue to Learn to Heal and Be Generous with myself so I can be generous with others.

Creating space in our lives for what is healthy and healing is the compost that feeds the whole garden and allows it to bloom.

How to Say No with Grace

Many people love the idea of saying no but worry about how others will react. We imagine possible future consequences like hurt feelings or disappointment, so we psych ourselves out by putting ourselves in charge of not only our own feelings, but other people's, too. We need to remind ourselves of the lessons the other Touchstones have taught us, and that it's actually pretty disrespectful to assume that other people can't handle a little disappointment and would rather have you lie to them. Would *you* want someone to spend an evening with you when they didn't want to? Exactly.

It's also not wrong to care about other people's feelings, but what we are managing is our own behavior and impact, best we can. A concept I learned from Robert Gass and Judith Ansara, who lead fabulous retreats for couples, is that when someone asks something of us, they are bidding for our affection and attention. It's an inherently vulnerable thing to do, so we want to respond with care. (By the way, if you've ever gone to couples' counseling, you already know that the stuff you learn there works in every part of your life. I highly recommend it!)

When someone asks me to do something that I either don't want to do or can't do, I respond first by saying thank you. Then, I don't burden them with the long list of reasons why I'm going to say no. I've learned that this is rarely for the other person's benefit—we do it to make ourselves feel better, but truly, no one really wants to hear it. Then, if appropriate, I can make a counteroffer that extends a yes on terms that I can meet.

Here's how that sounds with my husband (this is a real interaction, because do you know how many Spider-Man movies there are?):

> "Honey, can we make some popcorn and watch *Spider-Man: Into the Spider-Verse* tonight?"

> "Sweetie, thanks for asking, and I'd love to watch a movie with you tonight. I'm not up for watching a Spider Man movie, though. Can we see what else is on your list and find something we'd both like to watch?"

The most essential thing to remember is that our goal is to be truly honest. We must give our yes or no freely and mean it, drawing on our Touchstones to Honor Honesty and Walk in Integrity. A good way to check is to practice our answer in our heads and see if we feel an immediate twinge of resentment or reluctance. Check again to discern what you really mean to say.

Why does it matter to be honest about not wanting to watch Spider-Man (again)? What does this have to do with Imposter Syndrome and the topic of this chapter, Creating Space?

If I've had a tiring week and am looking forward to some downtime on Friday night, the last thing I want to do is feel resentful and like I wasted an evening doing something I don't enjoy. When I give my time and space for rejuvenation away, I leave myself open to being stressed, which makes me more susceptible to Imposter Syndrome.

When we lie with the small things in our personal or professional lives, we develop a habit that will spill over into the big things, too. We are trying to avoid being imposters in our own lives. We are striving for self-honesty. And, I can promise you that while my husband wishes that I loved Spidey as much as he does, he has no interest in being in a relationship with someone who lies and then resents him for it.

Guard and Protect Your Time

Think of something you have that is precious to you. It may be a macaroni necklace the kid you babysat in high school gave you when you left for college, or it may be a diamond-studded Rolex watch. Whatever it is, if it's precious, I'm guessing that you treat it with care. Would you hand it over to someone who didn't value it the way you do? Would you hand it over to someone just because you thought doing so would impress them or make them approve of you?

When we struggle with Imposter Syndrome, we often struggle to see our own value and worth. If we've bought into the story our ego tells us, our value is only as good as others' assessment of us. If we don't value ourselves, we can hand over our most precious of gifts—the very time of our lives. Our time is ours to steward, guard, and protect. No one else is responsible for doing that for us. We literally hold our life in our hands, for just this blink of an eye.

Steward it well.

It is so liberating to really know what I want, what truly makes me happy, what I will not tolerate. I have learned that it is no one else's job to take care of me but me.
—Beyonce Knowles-Carter

Touchstone Practice: Create Space

Start Small: Five-minute Moments

As a coach, one of the first things people say when we start talking about creating space is, "I just don't have time." So if you're thinking and believing that way in this moment, no problem. I encourage you to start small by creating what I like to call "Five-minute Moments."

I have yet to meet anyone, from a CEO to a parent of twin toddlers, who can't find five minutes for one of these restorative activities to get us out of our heads and into our bodies and emotions, at least once a day.

Set a timer for 5 minutes and then:

- Dance to your favorite playlist. (I still call them mixtapes - I'll always be a child of the '80's.)
- Go outside and look at the sky and clouds. Nothing else, just looking, no matter the weather.
- Do some yoga moves, calisthenics, or stretches.
- Wander around (outside or inside) without earbuds and notice what you see, hear, feel, and smell.
- Breathe in for four counts, out for four counts, repeat (for five minutes).
- Lay down and close your eyes. One muscle group at a time, tense up, then relax. Start at your head with your forehead, and work your way down your body. If there's a part of your body you can't move, imagine it tensing and relaxing.
- Take out some paper and a pencil and draw as many different kinds of boats that you can think of (without trying to be "artistic").

The possibilities are literally endless. See how many of your own you can come up with!

When you begin to string these Five-minute Moments together, day-by-day, you end up with a beautiful string of pearls that represent saying yes to yourself and relaxation for your mind, heart, body, and soul. Like brushing and flossing, each time matters.

Conclusion

Love liberates. It doesn't just hold — that's ego — love liberates!
—Dr. Maya Angelou

I'm feeling a flood of gratitude for you right now, for taking this journey through the Touchstones with me. I may not know your name, but I have felt your company during the hours I sat and wrote. You inspired me to keep writing when I was overcome with sadness, when I felt afraid to be vulnerable, when I wanted to stop looking honestly at the parts of myself and my life that I'm not proud of.

What kept me going was the realization that there is nothing I can say that you haven't also felt in some way. The details of our stories may be different, but we all know what it feels like to feel unworthy, to feel unlovable, to feel insecure, to feel we don't belong, to not trust ourselves, to not like ourselves.

I believe so deeply in our interdependent nature, that I believe I am you, and you are me. I feel no ownership of "my" story anymore, at age 51. In fact, I hold "my life" as simply a story, one of many that make up the world in which we coexist.

As I've mentioned before, for years, when people learned parts of my life story, they would say, "You really should write a book about your life." For years, I would say to myself, "I would love to write a book, but who'd be interested? What do I have to say that hasn't been said?"

In time, I began to listen with new ears and feel curious. What about my life story would lead someone to say it should be shared with the world? I realized that they felt the way

I do, which is best summed up in this quote from novelist William Nicholson: "We read to know we're not alone."

On a roadtrip many years ago, I was listening to an interview with activist and author Arundhati Roy who said, "Facts don't change people. Stories do." This quote has stayed with me ever since, and virtually everyone who knows me has heard me say it. I deeply believe this to be true. Books and stories were my lifeline to a better life, and so, if someone could be helped by my story, maybe I had a responsibility to generously share it rather than selfishly keep it hidden.

I wrote this book for every young person in pain, who feels trapped in a soul-crushing situation, who feels unlovable and unworthy. I wrote this book for every adult who still feels like that child, even though they may run a national organization and have a shelf full of awards. I wrote this book for every person who, because of their race or gender identity or sexual orientation or appearance or anything about them that doesn't conform to societal standards, feels like an imposter when they walk into a room.

Summary of the Ten Touchstones

Sometimes when I'm in a special place, there's a stone that calls out to me: Pick me up! I might find a stone while taking in the awe-inspiring view from a mountaintop after a breathtaking climb or while simply sitting by the lakeshore in the middle of the city, feeling contemplative. Some of the stones I have around my home have lost their stories, and I don't recall where or when I picked them up. Some stones I have around have great meaning for me still, like the purple rock from the top of a volcano at 15,000 ft in the Andes. I have a Touchstone right here by my keyboard from the shore of Lake Superior that is polished smooth and fits exactly in the cup of my palm, and I hold it for comfort when I'm in a stressful meeting or feeling less than confident in myself.

You now have Ten Touchstones in your pocket to take out and hold when Imposter Syndrome takes hold. Each Touchstone has a name and an essential lesson for overcoming the grip of Imposter Syndrome:

- Just Believe—allow yourself to live an expanded rather than a contracted life
- Develop Discernment—slow down, get really curious, and question your thoughts and beliefs
- Embrace Interdependence—mindfully cultivate our profound human need to be in relationship
- Be Generous—fill your own well first so you can pour a glass for others
- Learn to Heal—the only source of suffering is what we're thinking and believing
- Just Surrender— make friends with risking failure and not being in control so you can live without regret
- Be Brave and Courageous—have the courage to question, and you'll have all the courage you need to be free
- Walk in Integrity—to be at ease, live in alignment with your North Star guiding values and principles
- Honor Honesty—become trustworthy enough to tell the truth, first and foremost to yourself
- Create Space—become impeccable with your yes and no to steward the time of your life well

Paint them on stones and scatter them on your windowsill. Write them down and keep them in your backpack. Paint them on canvas and hang them in your bathroom by the mirror. Practice them until they are written on your heart, and you don't need the words anymore.

It's Never Too Late to Heal the Past

My writing coach, Dr. Jasmine Zapata, posed this question to me: If you could go back in time and talk to your 12-year-old self regarding the topic of overcoming Imposter Syndrome, what would you say?

When I first read that question, my eyes instantly welled up, and I began to cry. I cried for that hurt and hurting child, that girl who didn't deserve the abuse heaped on her head and heart. She didn't deserve to be hit and screamed at. She didn't deserve to be slapped across the room because she let the dog's water dish go dry. She didn't deserve a lifetime of insomnia because it wasn't safe to fall asleep. She didn't deserve her hunched shoulders and shame, and the wish that she could fly far away. She didn't deserve to believe she wasn't loved.

If I could go back in time, I would gather her in my arms and rock her. I would kiss her tears away and lay hands on all the places she hurt. I would lay my hand on her heart. I would tell her she's an innocent caught in a terrible situation. I would tell her, "It is not your fault." I would tell her that she has as much right to life and joy and safety as any other child, and that she doesn't have to do a single thing to earn love—she is lovable and worthy just as she is. I would tell her that hurt people hurt others, and she will be able to fly away one day.

I would tell her that she will heal, find people who will love and nurture her, and one day, she will learn to do that for herself. She will gather herself in her own arms and awaken to her true nature, which is love itself. I would tell her that even though she may think of herself as just a poor, scared girl from the cornfields, she will learn to see herself clearly as a strong, wise, worthy woman whose flaws make her wonderfully human, not undeserving and unworthy.

Stand Up and Show Your Soul

One of the most calming and powerful actions you can do to intervene in a stormy world is to stand up and show your soul. Struggling souls catch light from other souls who are fully lit and willing to show it.
—Dr. Clarissa Pinkola Estes

Just like others have said to me, the world needs *you* and your voice to help us catch light and find our way, together. As my mentor Cynthea Jones would often say, "The only thing worse than thinking that you don't matter is realizing that you do." That's a funny statement on first hearing, one that didn't make sense to me right away. What I now believe it to mean is that when I think I don't matter, I withhold myself from the world and play small, and in so doing, I make the world a more withholding and smaller place for others, too. I hope that after reading this book, you've found every reason to do all you can to overcome Imposter Syndrome. When we succumb to Imposter Syndrome, we literally diminish the world for all of us. As we are learning from the worldwide uprising against racial injustice, "your liberation is bound up with mine" (Lilla Watson). Who needs you to be free of Imposter Syndrome and shine as brightly as you can? We all do.

Right now, close your eyes and see the faces of all the people in your life, from your inner circle of loved ones, to the people you work with, to the people you buy your coffee and groceries from. How would you live if you knew that overcoming Imposter Syndrome in your life had the power to help them heal in their lives? The reality is that you do.

Heal Yourself, Heal Us All

I don't know you, but I have as much love for you as I do for myself, because these seemingly separate acts are one and the same. To put it another way, I finally understand the adage, "You can only love someone else as much as you love yourself." I used to disagree with this pearl of wisdom, arguing that I loved others more than myself because of how much I did for others, how self-sacrificing I was in order to serve others. It's so seductive, the idea of martyrdom and self-sacrifice as evidence of love. But now I understand that I cannot give to others what I cannot give to myself.

This is tricky to get my head around until I look at the opposite of this idea, which is that I will love others only as much as I love myself. How I treat myself is how I will treat you. If I judge myself harshly, I will judge you harshly. If I am not honest with myself, I will surely not be honest with others. If I think I'm undeserving and have to constantly prove myself worthy (e.g. Imposter Syndrome), I will expect you to prove yourself worthy, too.

If you take away only one lesson from this whole book, it is this: when we learn to accept and love ourselves, Imposter Syndrome will melt away, like winter snow in spring. When we are honest and truthful with ourselves, when we see ourselves clearly, when we understand our strengths as well as our flaws with equal clarity, we can't possibly be an imposter. We will be at home in whatever room, meeting, or office we find ourselves, because we are at home with ourselves.

You do not need to be perfect. You just need to be honest and courageous and true. You do not need to prove your worth. You are worthy just as you are. When you free yourself, you free the world.

We cannot begin to imagine what is lost to the world when we keep ourselves small and cower on the sidelines, in the shadows. The world needs your light—so *shine*.

> *"You yourself, as much as anybody in the entire universe, deserve your love and affection."*
> The Buddha

About the Author

Jennifer Wilson, M.A. is a transformational coach, consultant, facilitator, and educator. She courageously shares her own life experiences of overcoming a childhood affected by abuse, trauma, mental illness, and addiction to profoundly illustrate how we can learn to see who we truly are and free ourselves from self-limiting beliefs. A lifelong advocate for the environment and people who are marginalized by systemic oppression, Jennifer has worked with thousands of youth and adults, co-founded two high schools, and consulted with world-changing organizations such as The Obama Foundation, Sierra Club, and NRDC. She has practiced mindfulness meditation for over a decade and regularly goes to the wilderness to inspire her soul. You can connect with her at https://consultnewleaf.com/.

About the Publishing Support Services

Dr. Jasmine Zapata is an award winning author, speaker, radio personality, and public health physician. She is also the CEO and founder of Motivational M.D. Publishing which is a family owned business that helps aspiring authors publish books that heal, uplift, and inspire. Do you want to write a book? If so, you can connect with Motivational M.D. Publishing at https://imreadytolaunch.com.

Made in the USA
Middletown, DE
02 November 2020